150 activities that you and your child will love!

# Myleene Klass

## Things to **make** and **do** with your children

# THANK YOU TO …

The most amazing family anyone could wish to have envelop them: Lola, Granddad, Severine Berman, Jonathan Shalit, Simon Jones, Dolapo Alafe-Aluko, Nazli Alizadeh, the Fisher massive, Lauren Laverne, Graeme, Fergus and Mackie, Cousin John Cross and Gareth Thistleton, Hannah "Banoo" Ovenstone, Vanessa Guallar, Julie, Mark and Layla Armstrong-Hughes, Carryl and Joel Thomas, Katie Birtwistle, Michelle O'Clee, Lola Belen, Natasha Hambi, Kate Halfpenny and Linda Papadopoulos.

My working family: Orion, ROAR Global, Hackford Jones, BabyK at Mothercare, Myleene Klass for Littlewoods, Start-rite by Myleene Klass, Myleene Klass Nails for JML, Save the Children, John Stewart and Classic FM.

Karen Sullivan for working so awesomely hard, being so terrifically inspiring and for having the foresight to bribe me with cake to meet my deadlines.

To my little mermaids Ava and Hero,
love Mama

x x x

Ava, aged 5

Hero, aged 1³/₄

# CONTENTS

# INTRODUCTION

Hi, busy mums and dads! If you are anything like me, you probably feel pressure to keep your children entertained and want to make sure they are learning and "advancing" as well. There are, of course, lots of blogs, websites and classes out there, but that's where it all gets a bit fraught. With this book I wanted to create something that's different from what's already available – something more friendly, more like a manual that will allow you to just dip into any page to find a fun activity or game. It's designed to give you lots of ideas for things you can do with your children, both indoors and out, and often on the spur of the moment. If it saves you from wracking your brains and soothes frazzled nerves, then I will have succeeded.

Before I became a mum, I used to be a music teacher, so music and word games are my "thing". Other areas such as gardening and cooking often leave me feeling rather useless, so I set out to produce a book with *achievable* projects and ideas. You don't need to be a gourmet chef to cook with your kids, and it really doesn't matter whether you've built a den, planted a seed, created a papier-mâché mask or played hopscotch before. This is a book full of ideas and you can adapt them any way you see fit, on wet and sunny days, on long car journeys, those dreaded "I'm *bored*" moments when your children need a little stimulation, just before you tear your hair out.

I've had five years to think up most of the ideas; some are from my childhood, some come from friends and some are of my own devising, from playing with my own children. So you are in safe mummy hands. None of them are preachy or complicated, and most don't need a truckload of ingredients or special equipment. The one thing you will need, though, is your collective imaginations – and a sense of fun.

## Trust me, we can do this!

*Myleene*
*x*

# FOREWORD

Play is an integral part of healthy child development. In fact, it is recognised by the United Nations High Commission for Human Rights as a right of every child, up there with food and shelter, and for good reason. Children learn through play and it contributes to their well-being on all levels, including cognitively, socially, emotionally and physically. It also offers an ideal way for parents to engage with their children and to promote a relaxed, undemanding interaction with them.

Play is often under-rated by today's busy parents, many of whom go to great lengths to supply expensive, educational toys and a series of highly scheduled, enriching activities to keep their children stimulated and occupied. However, without time and space to dream, to imagine, create and explore their own interests and potential within an elastic time frame, and at their own pace, children can and do miss out on one of the key elements of a happy, nurturing childhood.

A recent survey found that traditional games, such as tag, dressing up or making a den, have been supplanted by costly toys and gadgets because of fears about health and safety, and a belief that playing should have a goal. Parents surveyed admitted to feeling "under pressure to be fun", and only a third take their children outside to play. One in seven admitted that they were anxious that they "don't know what they are doing" when playing with their children, often leaving them to their own devices.

Parents need to be able to play effortlessly and enthusiastically with their children, inside and out, without wracking their brains for ideas, or worrying about the positive advantages. They also need to know that everything from negotiating an obstacle course and dressing up to making a mask, growing a tomato plant and even sorting the socks has educational benefits that cannot be underestimated. Time spent with children, supporting their interests, their development, their marvellous sense of fun and uninhibited creativity and imagination, is not only rewarding but hugely beneficial for the emotional health of children, parents and the entire family dynamic.

This book is a compendium of wonderful, stimulating ideas to keep children happy, inspired and entertained. Most of the ideas in this book require little expenditure, simply some imagination and a willingness to relax and enjoy the fun.

Myleene knows first-hand what sparks a child's interest and keeps them stimulated, and this book is the product of her resolve to find ways for parents to enjoy the time they spend with their children, undertaking activities that are inspiring, interesting, easy to set up and, above all, fun for everyone involved. This timely, much-needed book will entertain and encourage children of all ages, and give parents the confidence and creativity they need to play and make the most of valuable time with their children. What's more, as they rediscover the "lost art" of playing, parents will witness, first-hand, the enormous developmental benefits it delivers, and the happiness and well-being that ensue.

*Karen Sullivan*

CHILDCARE EXPERT
**BSC (HONS) DEVELOPMENTAL PSYCHOLOGY**
**MSC EDUCATIONAL PSYCHOLOGY**

# DEVELOPMENT ICONS

Children learn best through play, on all sorts of levels, and you may be surprised by the developmental milestones that they achieve without even being aware of it. While this book is not about pushing children forward or even ensuring that every activity or game they undertake is educational, I have worked with a child development specialist to show you what they are learning and the areas in which they will be developing. Knowing that your children are being stimulated in a productive way while they have fun is a huge relief – for me, anyway!

Most of the development icons are self-explantory, but a rule of thumb to follow with your child's motor skills developement is: Fine motor skills refers to the small muscles in the body and assist with everything from writing, eating and even doing up clothing. Gross motor skills refer to the larger muscles in the body, and assist with everything from balance, walking, lifting and throwing.

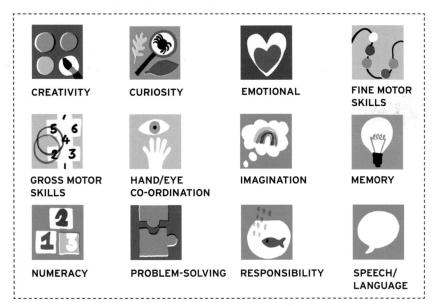

CREATIVITY

CURIOSITY

EMOTIONAL

FINE MOTOR SKILLS

GROSS MOTOR SKILLS

HAND/EYE CO-ORDINATION

IMAGINATION

MEMORY

NUMERACY

PROBLEM-SOLVING

RESPONSIBILITY

SPEECH/ LANGUAGE

# A B

# STORY
# TIME

**B**edtime is a magical time for me as I get to sit with both girls on my lap and just read. We read anything and everything in our house, from cartons in the refrigerator and labels on boxes to signs on the road - you name it, we read it. It is so important to focus on words and the sounds that comprise them on every possible occasion. It improves children's vocabularies, their speech and pronunciation, and it also stimulates their imaginations. We've got books galore, and in particular, I love ones with lots of rhymes and a strong rhythm. My girls love it when I "do the voices" in our stories, although Ava has started picking me up on my inconsistent accents. She's like my vocal coach!

If you don't have much time on your hands, the single most important thing you can do is spend time reading to your children. Those precious hours spent snuggled up, sharing an imaginary world, are unbeatable for bonding, emotional and cognitive development and, of course, happy memories.

In this chapter you will find ideas for activities based around words and reading to encourage language development, story sense and early reading skills. They will also help stimulate creativity and imagination, and introduce your child to the wonderful world of words, books and reading.

*Myleene*
*x*

# Story time suggestions

- *The Lorax, The Cat in the Hat* and *Oh, The Places You'll Go!* by Dr. Seuss

- *The Very Hungry Caterpillar* by Eric Carle

- *Esio Trot* by Roald Dahl

- *The Gruffalo* by Julia Donaldson

- *Pants* by Nick Sharratt

- *Goodnight Moon* by Margaret Wise Brown and Clement Hurd (for babies)

- *Slinky Malinki* by Lynley Dodd

- *Giraffes Can't Dance* by Giles Andreae and Guy Parker-Rees

- *One Snowy Night* (a Percy the Park Keeper story) by Nick Butterworth

- *Funnybones* by Janet and Allan Ahlberg

- *Don't Wake the Bear, Hare!* by Steve Smallman and Caroline Pedler

- *Dogger* by Shirley Hughes (old-school, but enchanting)

- *Mister Magnolia* by Quentin Blake

# TAKING TURNS

All you need is a book or a magazine, and most importantly, your imagination.

## WHAT TO DO:

**PICTURE BY PICTURE:** Try this activity with a children's magazine or a picture book. Open it up at random and make up a story based upon the first image that you see. Turn the page and encourage your child to continue the story based on the next image you come to. Continue like this until your story is complete or you've run out of pictures. This is particularly good fun when you have a magazine with a good selection of different advertisements and editorial features . . . you'll have to use your combined imaginations to get the various episodes in the story to link together coherently.

**TWISTS AND TURNS:** You can play this game without any visual prompts. Begin by setting the scene for your story and choosing a central character, all drawn from your imagination. Then ask your child to continue. When they've finished the next scene, it's your turn again. If your child finds this activity difficult at the outset, try giving them a few clues. Does the bear get lost in the woods? Who might be looking for him? How is he feeling? Is it night-time? What do you think he might do next? We often play this game in the car. It keeps everyone occupied thinking about how the story might unfold. Be prepared for your story to take some astonishing twists and surreal turns.

# 2

# MAKING YOUR OWN "LIFT-THE-FLAP" BOOK

Young children love lift-the-flap books and they also love the familiar - the people and places they know. Help your child to create their own storybook with pictures of favourite characters, farm animals or family photographs.

## WHAT TO DO:

Tape or staple several pieces of paper together to create a short book of around six pages. Cut out pictures from a magazine or use some family photos and paste them in the book. Conceal a part of each picture by taping a flap of paper over it. Your child might like to do some drawings around the pictures and on the flaps to make it more colourful.

Now, sit down with your child and work out a story based on the images. The idea is to create a cliffhanging sentence or a "who could it be" moment for each page to encourage them to lift the flap to find out who or what's underneath. There's no need to write any text. When they know the story off by heart create a new one, or select some more images and make a new book.

# WHAT COMES NEXT?

Most children love having stories read to them and latch on to one or two that they ask for or listen to again and again.

WHAT TO DO:
This simple activity can be based around a favourite book. When you come to the end of every page, ask your little one what comes next. If they're familiar with the book they will probably be able to tell you exactly what takes place on the next page. Or choose a new book and ask them to use their imagination to decide what comes next. It will encourage story sense – i.e., the idea that in a book events unfold in such a way that every page brings something new, and there is a beginning, middle and end to a narrative.

# MY FAMILY ALBUM

This is similar to the lift-the-flap activity, but for older children. One of the ways children learn to read is by creating stories based on the pictures they see in books. Or you could try creating stories based on the family, as it will be more personal. It will also help to keep those memories crystal clear and the creative juices flowing.

WHAT TO DO:
Create a small album with photos of just you and your family, including your little one, of course. Use a range of photos, taken across the years if possible. Ask your child to paste them in the book in a particular order, grouping them by family member, or chronologically; they can label them too if they like.

When the album is complete, use it as a basis for telling stories about the family. Children love hearing tales about themselves – and about parents or grandparents, aunts and uncles – the naughtier the better! Looking at a picture of you when you were younger (bad hair day included!), your child can make up a story based on where you were photographed and what you were wearing. Encourage them to tell a story about themselves as a baby, or to recall a favourite memory or activity that has been captured in a photograph. The idea is to encourage them to remember things about the events and people in the photos, or, if the photos were taken before they were born, to use their imagination to dream up stories based on them.

# "FEARS AND FABLES" ROLE PLAY

Use the power of stories to help prepare your child for new events and experiences. Placing imaginary characters in stories centred around particular issues that your child finds difficult or daunting will help them to become more resourceful, positive and independent.

## WHAT TO DO:

When your child is about to experience something for the first time that you believe could cause them concern, or for which you simply want to prepare them, it's a nice idea to make up a story about it. For example, if you are expecting a new baby, or your little one is due to start at a new school or nursery, create an imaginary version of the same scenario with another little boy or girl at the heart of it. This distances your child from the suggestion that they may be worried or anxious, and also gives them an opportunity to add their own input, ask questions or express fears.

Stories about characters experiencing events that your child might find difficult can help to make them more independent, such as the little girl who had a lovely first day at nursery, the teddy bear who found a best friend at school, or the boy who crossed the road safely with the lollipop lady. This approach to tackling children's concerns offers plenty of scope, and your child may even want reassuring stories to be repeated over and over again. Stories can also be an important means of communicating with children who may not have the emotional resources or verbal capacity to convey things that are on their mind. If you get into the habit of asking your child what they'd like a story to be about, you may gain some insight into their thoughts and feelings.

It's also a nice idea to use stories to battle "demons". For example, if your child is afraid of the dark, there's no point in saying that there's nothing to be scared of. Instead, create a story in which a child becomes a hero or heroine, banishing lurking beasties, or whatever is frightening them, with a magic potion made with a splash of mum's perfume, the peel of half an orange and a tiny bit of fur from their favourite teddy, all mixed with water in a bottle with a spray top. One spray and the baddies are history! Sounds crazy? Just wait, your child will probably want to experiment with their own concoctions to save the day. By creating an imaginary scenario for a problem, you will also instil the idea that solutions can be found. In this way your child will learn to problem-solve on their own.

# FUN GAMES TO ENCOURAGE READING

Here are several easy games designed to help and encourage your child to read. You'll find a few others dotted elsewhere in the book.

## FILL IN THE BLANKS:
When your child becomes familiar with a story, try missing out some words the next time you read it and encourage your little one to fill in the blanks. It will help with sequencing and make your child part of the story telling. Books that rhyme make this easier.

**FOR EXAMPLE:**
"Hairy Maclary from Donaldson's _____ "
(from *Hairy Maclary* by Lynley Dodd)

**OR**

"I do not like Green Eggs and Ham, I do not like them _____ "
(from *Green Eggs and Ham* by Dr. Seuss)

## EVERYDAY READING AND WRITING:
Encourage your little one to write short notes or messages to help you around the home. Your "to do" list, a note for the milkman, a reminder to daddy to collect the cat from the vet. If your child isn't writing yet, they can draw the note in pictures instead. They will still be learning the basics of writing and self-expression and it won't be long before they're asking you to spell out words for them. Go at your little one's pace and give them lots of opportunity (and pencils and paper) to practise their writing.

## WRITE STORIES TOGETHER:

Even the youngest children will have ideas for stories, so offer to "take dictation", write them on a couple of sheets of paper and staple them into a book. Get children to illustrate their tales with lots of colourful artwork. Older children may be able to write a basic story by themselves, but you can help by teaching them how a story works, explaining that it has a setting, characters, a beginning and an end, and ideally a plot. Teaching children to think out their stories in advance of writing them down is a good way to encourage them to focus and to consider their ideas.

Alternatively, you can write a story in a book, but leave lots of blanks for your little one to fill in.

**FOR EXAMPLE:**

"It was a _____ day in _____, and the tiny _____ shivered as the _____ blew."

Why not keep an ongoing story notebook, adding a few sentences every day? You could write one page and your child writes the next. If teaching children about verbs, adjectives and basic grammar seems too much like a school lesson, remember that when children enjoy an activity, such as a pleasurable exercise shared with a parent, they are much more likely to understand and retain information, and be able to apply it successfully at a later date.

## MAKE SPELLING FUN:

You need a set of letters of the alphabet for this game – such as Scrabble® pieces, a set of alphabet cards (which are easy to make if you don't have a set), alphabet refrigerator magnets or bath sponges. The game is to race to see who can make words the most quickly. Pick out a few letters and move them around to make different words. How many words can you make from the letters "A", "B" and "T"? Tab? Bat? Is "Abt" a real word? A point for discussion and some fun.

## I SAW IT FIRST:

This is a good game to play with several children and even little ones can play. Write all the letters of the alphabet on small bits of paper or card (one letter per card) and pop them into a bag. The children take turns to retrieve a letter and say the sound of it out loud ("ah" for "A" and "buh" for "B". . .). The first person to find something in the room that starts with that letter wins that round and takes the next go. Continue until all the letters are used up, or you all run out of steam.

# TELL ME AGAIN!

We all know what it's like ... even after the longest, most involved story session comes the inevitable demand to "Read it again!" Children love repetition and it's one of the best tools for encouraging learning. But even the most engaging of children's tales begin to pale after the umpteenth reading, so this is one way to solve the problem and get your child to take an active part in the story at the same time.

WHAT TO DO:
You don't need to be a techno genius to make a recording these days. Smart phones and MP3 players make it easy, or tape recorders can still do the job the more old-fashioned way. Start by reading the story in the usual way – a conventional reading will be perfect for playing after the bedtime play and just as your little one is drifting off to sleep. Then record a different version, this time leaving out words of the narrative for your little one to fill in (see pages 22–23).

Or try another version in which your child plays one of the characters and fills in some of the gaps in speech, saying several words or whole phrases "in character". If your child is very young, choose a character that doesn't have too many words to say. Ask them to make animal noises in a favourite farmyard tale, or some background sound effects (some whooshing of the wind or the clip-clop of a horse). Have fun with your recordings, and make them as personal (or as silly) as you wish. Not only will you both enjoy making them, but your child will have a new relaxing and enjoyable soundtrack to fall asleep to.

# Fairy tales

Albert Einstein said, "If you want your children to be intelligent, read them fairy tales. If you want them to be more intelligent, read them more fairy tales". It's not often that I quote Einstein, but I tend to agree with him. Fairy tales have had pretty bad press over the past decade, with feminists up in arms at the idea that women are always waiting around for Prince Charming to save the day, and at times I have agreed with them in the more extreme, desperate tales. However, there have been moves to make these stories more politically correct, which has undermined much of what it is about them that enthrals children and captivates their imaginations.

For one thing, fairy tales help children to be resourceful. Yes, really! Every fairy tale has some sort of hurdle or problem that must be overcome by a central character. Dragons are slayed, wicked stepmothers get their comeuppance, dark forests are negotiated and wolves outwitted, not by a twist of fate or a lottery win but through determination, perserverance and goodness. I like that. I also like the fact that the good guy or girl always wins. There is absolutely no harm in teaching children that goodness prevails. Similarly, there are deep-seated morals in every story, which provide the basis for some good discussions.

Fairy tales also help children to face fears. It is nonsense to suggest that these stories create fears; many children are naturally afraid of the dark, monsters, ghosts, witches and all sorts of things. Reading about them, all snuggled up in bed with a parent, and seeing the bad guys and monsters challenged and overcome is healthy. When they are faced with issues and fears of their own, a small seed will have been planted in their minds telling them that these too can be resolved and beaten.

Fairy tales also provide *huge scope* for a child's imagination. What could be more exciting than a world that is completely different from their own? A whole world that is concealed inside a tree trunk or that is inhabited by fairies or scary creatures, a country beneath the sea or a place where everything is frozen and the sun never shines? These stories inspire imagination and fantasy; the building blocks of creativity.

If it really bothers you that Sleeping Beauty has to be awoken by Prince Charming, then put the prince to bed and get Princess Merida (*Brave*) to wake him up instead. Some of the original stories are also quite gory, so you may need to use your discretion and tone them down here and there, depending on the sensitivity of your child. Or just blatantly change the ending like I often do. The princess lives happily ever after and hangs out with her girlfriends! However, in essence the stories are unmatched in their ability to appeal to children and to stimulate their imagination.

You'll have your own favourites, but if you haven't read all of the following to your children, now is the time.

- Cinderella
- Little Red Riding Hood
- The Elves and the Shoemaker
- Jack and the Beanstalk
- The Boy Who Cried Wolf
- The Three Little Pigs
- The Princess and the Pea
- Sleeping Beauty
- Rapunzel
- Snow-White and Rose-Red
- The Ugly Duckling
- Rumpelstiltskin
- Hansel and Gretel
- The Little Match Girl
- The Emperor's New Clothes
- The Snow Queen
- Puss in Boots

And although I hate to say "there is an app for that", there are some award-winning applications that not only retell the very best stories, but also provide educational games to help children learn from them.

SEE PAGE 233 FOR MORE DETAILS.

# MAKING MUSIC

**M**usic has always played a very important role in my life. I started to learn the piano at the age of four, and I truly believe that it's helped me with everything, from co-ordination and creativity to basic maths and working in a team. Music-making isn't restricted to conventional instruments; it's all around us – the rhythmic dripping of a tap, tyres bumping along a road, the clanging of the lid of a bin as it shuts, the sharp rattle of a teacup in its saucer on a train journey. Music is everywhere. Encourage children to listen out for the taps, bangs and clangs, and the tones and rhythms in their everyday life.

When listening to a piece of what we regard as conventional music it's very important to engage your children's interest. Dragging children along to music lessons that they don't enjoy is simply no fun for anyone, children or teacher. Trust me on this one; I've been there in both roles. Instead, let them explore, experiment, appreciate and enjoy. Try to use music in different ways. For example, when Ava had to remember the complicated name of a dinosaur, we helped her by making up a song about it. Music can help the learning process on various levels, perhaps because it approaches learning from a different angle and therefore helps information both to sink in more quickly and to stay there.

Music of all kinds can play a role in your children's lives. Encourage them to listen to a wide spectrum – pop, jazz and classical. Classical music in particular is thought by some (including me) to enhance intellect and stimulate development. Classical pieces can seem intimidating if you aren't familiar with them, but the key is to remember that there is no right or wrong way to respond to them. Listen to a piece with your child and make up a story to go with it; what moods and feelings does it evoke: calm, joy, tension? Does it sound like birds celebrating the arrival of spring, dramatic waves crashing on a shore, trolls and goblins marching through a mountain cavern? Above all, allow children to listen and respond to music, whether it soothes or energises them. Make music a part of daily life as often as you can, and you are bound to see results.

*Myleene*
*x*

# Songs to get you started

- Twinkle, Twinkle, Little Star (Yes, this is classical music; it was composed by Mozart)

- The Carnival of the Animals (Aquarium, Fossils, The Swan) by Saint-Saëns

- The Blue Danube by Johann Strauss (real old-school stuff)

- In the Hall of the Mountain King by Edvard Grieg

- Night on the Bare Mountain by Mussorgsky

- Peter and the Wolf by Sergei Prokofiev (great for storytelling and learning about the sounds of different instruments)

- William Tell Overture by Rossini

- Clair de Lune by Debussy (wonderful music about the moon)

- Soundtrack from *Pirates of the Caribbean* by Hans Zimmer/ Klaus Badelt

- The Young Person's Guide to the Orchestra by Benjamin Britten

- The Beyondness of Things by John Barry (Hero sings along to this!)

- Soundtrack from *E.T.* by John Williams

- Candide by Leonard Bernstein

## Now, it's up to you to enjoy and explore!

# MUSIC MOODS

Music and movement provide children with an outlet for expressing their feelings and moods. Listening to or playing different types of music with your little one also provides an opportunity to discuss different emotions. Giving feelings a "label" is an important part of children's emotional development, and learning to use music to reflect or even change your child's mood will prove invaluable.

## WHAT TO DO:

Pick a time when your child is ready to play. Choose different types of music, such as lullabies or relaxing classical pieces, up-tempo rock or hip-hop, traditional nursery rhymes, waltzes, salsa. Dance to the music or simply sit and listen. Talk about how the music makes you both feel: Silly? Happy? Sleepy? Relaxed? Excited?

Why not create a special dance to go with a favourite piece of music? Or choose a gentle, relaxing song that you can sing together when it's bedtime or time for your child's nap? (see page 41). Try adding your own instruments. Shake a rattle or some maracas, bang a drum or some pots and pans, tinkle away on a xylophone or keyboard. The idea is to introduce music to daily life in a positive, interactive way, and to use it to express feelings. Regular "musical conversations" are a lovely way to keep in touch with your child's emotions.

# NOISY CLOTHES LINE

Using sturdy clothes pegs, twist ties or pipe cleaners, attach a variety of different musical instruments or "sound-makers" along a stretch of extended clothes line. Good choices include rattles, bells, wind chimes, maracas, empty pots or tins, plastic cups, and even sheets of aluminium foil, which will all make a satisfying noise when struck, but make sure your child is able to reach them.

Arm your little one with a stick or a wooden or metal spoon with a long handle and they can now bash away to their heart's content. Or try aiming a garden hose at the instruments, and see how much noise (and music) you can make by playing the water jet across them. Or sit back and let the wind create its own gentle sounds.

# WATER MUSIC

Fill a series of jars with different amounts of water to give each a unique sound when struck. Create your own "water symphony" and teach your child about pitch at the same time. The more water there is in the jar, the lower the pitch of the sound that will be produced. Less water means the pitch will be higher. My girls love this activity and I think it's a fantastic way to explain volume and pitch.

## WHAT YOU'LL NEED:
- **Glass jars or bottles (6-10 will provide a variety of sounds in different pitches)**
- **Water**
- **Sticky labels and felt-tip pen**
- **1 spoon per person**

## WHAT TO DO:
Place the jars on a firm, flat surface, in a row, with a small space between each one. Fill each jar with a different amount of water, starting with just a small amount in the first jar, adding a little more to each as you move along the row. Ask your child to tap each jar gently with a spoon and listen carefully to the different pitches of sound they produce. Attach a sticky label to each and number them from one to ten (or however many jars you have). One for the highest sound and ten for the lowest. The jars should already be in order of pitch, from high to low, left to right.

Experiment with moving the jars around in a different order and tap them in their new sequence to see what lovely sounds you can create. Or you play the high notes while your child plays the low ones. See if you can play a familiar tune together.

# BIG BOX, LITTLE DRUMMER

Banging away at a drum is an excellent way for your child to burn off a little energy and develop a sense of rhythm. It couldn't be easier to make this drum kit.

## WHAT YOU'LL NEED:
- **4-5 boxes of varying sizes, square boxes or round boxes are ideal**
- **Coloured paper and/or stickers**
- **Sticky tape and craft glue**
- **Scissors**
- **1 metal saucepan lid**
- **2 chunky, unsharpened pencils (or a pair of wooden spoons) for drumsticks**

## WHAT TO DO:
Tape down the lids of the boxes and turn them upside down (so that the lids are on the ground). Decorate the boxes with stickers, bits of coloured paper or anything else that makes them look suitably bright and festive.

Arrange the boxes in a circle on the ground. Smaller boxes can be placed on a small chair or stool to raise them up a little. Put the saucepan lid on top of one of the taller boxes to make a cymbal. Your child can sit or stand in front of the drum kit and, using the "drumsticks", bang away to their heart's content. Put on some music and encourage them to play along, matching the beat when they can. Change the tempo of the music every now and then to see if your child can keep up!

# RAINSTICKS

Rainsticks were used by many Native American tribes to encourage rainfall. When turned upside down the contents trickle through the foil "snake" inside, making a satisfying, soothing sound like rain. Decorate with paper or stickers. The more colourful the better.

## WHAT YOU'LL NEED:

- Cardboard tube (kitchen roll tubes are perfect)
- Aluminium foil
- Scissors
- Strong brown parcel paper
- Sticky tape and craft glue
- Dry rice or beans
- Coloured paper and/or stickers

## WHAT TO DO:

Place the cardboard tube on the table. Cut two lengths of foil roughly the same length as the tube. Roll each one up to form a "snake" and scrunch it up a little. Twist the ends of the two snakes together at the top and then wind each one around the other loosely, and twist the two bottom ends together to form the filter. Insert the foil filter into the cardboard tube.

Next, cut out two circles of brown paper, about 4cm wider than the width of the tube. Place one of the circles over one end of the tube, and carefully fold down the excess paper around the top. Tape it in position securely. Turn the tube over and pour some dry rice or beans down around the filter until the tube is about one-third full. Take the second circle of brown paper and place it over the other end of the tube, fold down the excess paper and tape it in position. Decorate the tube with coloured paper and stickers. Slowly turn the rainstick upside down and then back again. Does it sound like falling rain?

# THE BIG PAN BAND

A saucepan band is an easy way to make music almost instantly. Just choose a few metal saucepans of different sizes from the kitchen cupboard, place them upside down on a firm surface and encourage your little one to bash away with a selection of different "drumsticks". Metal serving spoons, spatulas and wooden spoons all make different but satisfying, fun sounds. Bang two saucepan lids together like a cymbal, or place some unpopped popcorn or rice in a small saucepan, tape down the lid firmly, and get shaking, maraca-style.

Play some music in the background or sing along with your child's performance. Making music of any description allows your child to engage in rhythm and movement activities, helping to synchronise brain and body and develop co-ordination. It also has a direct effect on the parts of the brain that control speech, language, memory and emotions. Children learn and develop while having fun.

# GUITAR HERO

This home-made guitar makes good use of items from the recycling box and provides a great opportunity to make music at the same time. Make sure you choose strong elastic bands so that they don't snap if your child gets too carried away.

## WHAT YOU'LL NEED:

- **Empty rectangular tissue box**
- **Scissors**
- **Cardboard tube (kitchen roll tubes are perfect)**
- **Sticky tape and/or craft glue**
- **Paints and brush, felt-tip pens, coloured paper and stickers**
- **Elastic bands of different thicknesses, large enough to slip around the box lengthways**

## WHAT TO DO:

Enlarge the opening in the box slightly with scissors if necessary – this will form the guitar's sound hole. Place one end of the cardboard tube over the centre of one end of the box and draw around it. Cut out the circle and insert the tube into the hole to form the guitar neck. Push the tube about 3cm into the box and glue or tape it in position. Now paint the guitar or decorate with coloured paper or stickers.

When the paint and glue is dry, slip the elastic bands around the tissue box lengthways. Make sure they are positioned in order of thickness, with the thickest at the top and the thinnest at the bottom. Place an even number on each side of the guitar neck, they should sit nicely over the sound hole. The different thicknesses of elastic bands will produce different sounds. Now all budding guitar heroes can start strumming away.

# PAPER PLATE TAMBOURINES

A brightly coloured paper plate tambourine will make a lovely jingly sound when your child rattles and shakes it. Why not form your own marching band with tambourines and drums, and some good old-fashioned stomping in time to the music?

## WHAT YOU'LL NEED:
- **2 paper plates**
- **Hole punch**
- **Paint or coloured felt-tip pens, glitter, stickers**
- **Craft glue**
- **5 large jingle bells**
- **Pipe cleaners or twist ties**

## WHAT TO DO:
Place the plates on top of each other and punch five holes, at regular intervals, around the rim of the plates. To decorate the backs of the plates, place them face down on a work surface and paint or colour them, adding glitter and stickers to create bright patterns. Once dry, glue the plates together, face-to-face, so that the decorated backs face outwards and the holes are perfectly aligned. Leave to dry.

While they are drying, prepare the bells. Thread a 5cm length of pipe cleaner or a twist tie through the tiny ring at the end of each bell and twist to secure it. Attach a bell to each of the holes in the tambourine, threading the pipe cleaner or twist tie through the hole and twisting both ends together to secure it in place. Your tambourine is complete!

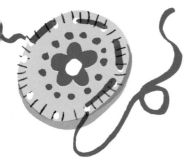

# MUSICAL BINGO

Even if you are not very familiar with the sounds that different musical instruments make, you can help your child learn to recognise them as well as learn to identify them yourself at the same time. CDs sampling the sounds of different instruments are available in shops or online. Listen to one together and mime playing each instrument. Look for pictures of the instruments in books or on the Internet, and when you are both feeling more confident, try this game of musical bingo.

Cut out pictures of six or nine common instruments and glue them to a piece of card to create a bingo sheet, arranging them in two or three rows. Make a bingo card for each player. Using large buttons for markers, play one of your favourite pieces of instrumental music (*Young Person's Guide to the Orchestra* is a good one for this game, or a movie soundtrack such as *Pirates of the Caribbean*) and place a marker on the picture of the instrument you hear. The first one to spot a particular instrument puts down their marker and the first one to fill a line or the whole card wins. You'll both become faster and more adept at picking up the sounds as your knowledge increases. It's a fun way of introducing your child to the stimulating world of music.

I love taking every opportunity to train my children's ears to the sounds of different instruments. When we were in Egypt recently, we came across someone playing a "shawm" and the girls were genuinely excited to hear something new.

# I'VE GOT RHYTHM!

Clapping, marching and banging in time to a beat will teach your child about rhythm and patterns, which helps with language and reading. Learning about patterns also teaches children how things work together and allows them to predict what comes next in a sequence. But best of all, it's good, noisy fun and encourages concentration and memory skills.

WHAT TO DO:
Try clapping a simple rhythm and ask your child to repeat it. See how many claps your child can manage. Turn it into a game by asking them to clap a rhythm for you to copy and repeat. Or bang out a rhythm pattern on your Big Box Drum Kit (see page 34), or just stomp around in a marching rhythm. Clap out the syllables of each other's names: Mum-my, Jon-a-than, etc. Clap or march to favourite nursery rhymes and songs such as Row, Row, Row Your Boat. When you've become really adept, how about clapping out the first line or chorus of a song and trying to guess it?

# SING ALONG, SLEEPY HEAD

Help your little one to wind down at the end of the day with a gentle song played every night before bedtime.

## WHAT TO DO:

Repetition aids learning and encourages an understanding of routine, which also helps children to feel secure. If you have a favourite bedtime lullaby, why not record it, with both of you singing along? It's a lovely way to keep track of your child's development (not to mention singing skills) and can also be useful to help calm and relax children when they're feeling under the weather, need a little reassurance to settle, or when you are away from home.

Alternatively, what about a jolly song to help wake you up and get you both going in the morning? Choose something that makes you feel lively and happy and gets your day off to a positive start. Getting children involved in choosing music that affects them in different ways helps them to express their emotions and encourages music appreciation; they can often surprise you with their unexpected song choices. What could be a better way to start and end the day than with music!

# LET ME SHOW YOU!

Kids like nothing better than showing off their "moves". Take advantage of their natural enthusiasm and energy by creating an exercise or dance routine to music, and then film it. The video clip will also make a good addition to your Memory Box (see page 92). This is the perfect opportunity for role reversal, allowing your child to teach you for a change.

WHAT TO DO:
Play some favourite tunes, and get your child to do some exercises to the music, such as star jumps, hops, skips, roly-polys, touch-your-toes, whatever they feel like. Ask them to explain what they're doing as they jump about, to create the perfect new fitness video!

If your child likes dancing, ask them to create a dance routine and film it. Again, if they can provide a running commentary explaining how to do the dance, or even just sing along to the music, even better. You can play the pupil or demonstrate a few of your own moves, if your child runs out of ideas.

Great for co-ordination, flexibility and motor control, this fun activity also provides all the benefits of exercise when you can't go outside. It's also a fun way to encourage your child to learn to move to music and to develop their co-ordination skills.

# 20 ACTION RHYMES AND SONGS

Action rhymes not only encourage co-ordination and listening skills, they also help with sequencing, memory and language development. And they can help to instil a love of music too. Set aside some time every day to act out your favourite songs. They are also an ideal way to keep small children occupied on car journeys.

# IF YOU'RE HAPPY AND YOU KNOW IT

This action song is perfect for children of all ages. Even babies can take part, if you clap their hands together and stamp their little feet for them. This is Hero's favourite and very popular in our household.

If you're happy and you know it, clap your hands
If you're happy and you know it, clap your hands
If you're happy and you know it, and you really want to show it
If you're happy and you know it, clap your hands

If you're happy and you know it, stamp your feet
If you're happy and you know it, stamp your feet
If you're happy and you know it, and you really want to show it
If you're happy and you know it, stamp your feet

If you're happy and you know it, shout "Hurray!"
If you're happy and you know it, shout "Hurray!"
If you're happy and you know it, and you really want to show it
If you're happy and you know it, shout "Hurray!"

If you're happy and you know it, do all three
If you're happy and you know it, do all three
If you're happy and you know it, and you really want to show it
If you're happy and you know it, do all three

# HEADS, SHOULDERS, KNEES AND TOES

This energetic rhyme gets little children moving faster and faster, as you repeat it faster and faster. You can also leave blanks in place of some of the words, and see if they can remember what to do next. For example, "**Head, shoulders, _____ and toes!**" Great for learning the different parts of the body, co-ordination and memory, this song appeals to children of all ages.

Head, shoulders, knees and toes, knees and toes
Head, shoulders, knees and toes, knees and toes
And eyes and ears and mouth and nose
Head, shoulders, knees and toes, knees and toes

# THE GRAND OLD DUKE OF YORK

This traditional nursery rhyme has a strong marching rhythm, which is perfect to get little feet stamping and arms waving. The idea is to stand up, sit down and stand halfway up at the appropriate points. The lyrics are easy to remember and your little one will have to move fast to keep up!

Oh, the grand old Duke of York
He had ten thousand men
He marched them up to the top of the hill
And he marched them down again

And when they were up, they were up
And when they were down, they were down
And when they were only halfway up
They were neither up nor down

# WIND THE BOBBIN UP

This is a traditional nursery rhyme that dates back to the 1890s. It's perfect for even young children, as its simple movements and melody make it easy to remember and perform. This is Ava's favourite!

Wind the bobbin up
Wind the bobbin up
Pull, pull, clap, clap, clap
Wind the bobbin up
Wind the bobbin up
Pull, pull, clap, clap, clap
Point to the ceiling, point to the floor
Point to the window, point to the door
Clap your hands together, one two three
Put your hands upon your knee

Wind it back again
Wind it back again
Pull, pull, clap, clap, clap
Wind it back again
Wind it back again
Pull, pull, clap, clap, clap
Point to the ceiling, point to the floor
Point to the window, point to the door
Clap your hands together, one two three
Put your hands upon your knee

# INCY WINCY SPIDER

Sometimes called "Itsy Bitsy spider" but whatever version you use,
all children enjoy performing this spidery tale.

Incy Wincy spider climbed up the water spout
Down came the rain and washed poor Incy out
Out came the sunshine and dried up all the rain
And Incy Wincy spider climbed up the spout again

# RING-A-RING O'ROSES

It has wrongly been suggested that this rhyme refers to the plague,
with sneezing children mimicking collapsing in illness on the spot. In fact,
it was written long after the end of the plague and is believed to be
a simple, playful rhyme designed merely to entertain children.

Ring-a-ring o'roses,
A pocket full of posies
A-tishoo! A-tishoo!
We all fall down

Ashes in the water
Ashes in the sea
We all jump up
With a one two three

# ROW, ROW, ROW, YOUR BOAT

**Sit your child in between your legs, facing you, and row together in time to this song. The first verse is traditional, while the following ones have been designed to make children laugh!**

Row, row, row your boat
Gently down the stream
Merrily, merrily, merrily, merrily
Life is but a dream

Row, row, row your boat
Gently down the stream
If you see a crocodile
Don't forget to scream

Row, row, row your boat
Gently down the river
If you see a polar bear
Don't forget to shiver

Row, row, row your boat
Gently to the shore
If you see a lion there
Don't forget to roar

# THIS IS THE WAY THE LADY RIDES

The lyrics to this old favourite vary quite dramatically between versions, so you can adjust the words as you see fit. Seat your child on your knee and bounce them up and down in time with the rhyme, then slide them off gently in the final verse.

This is the way the lady rides
Clippity-clop, clippity-clop
This is the way the lady rides
Clippity-clop, clippity-clop

This is the way the gentleman rides
Gallopy-trot, gallopy-trot
This is the way the gentleman rides
Gallopy-trot, gallopy-trot

This is the way the huntsman rides
Gallopy-gallopy, gallopy-gallopy!
This is the way the huntsman rides
Gallopy-gallopy, gallopy-gallopy!

This is the way the old man rides,
Hobbledy . . . hobbledy . . .
fall in the ditch!

# ROCK-A-BYE BABY

**Rock a pretend baby in your arms, or choose one of you child's favourite dollies. Not surprisingly, young children *love* the idea of a baby falling out of a tree!**

Rock-a-bye baby, in the treetop
When the wind blows, the cradle will rock
When the bough breaks, the cradle will fall
And down will come baby, cradle and all

# TWO LITTLE BLACKBIRDS

**Use your fingers to create your birds, and hide them behind your back when they "fly away"! This is great for hand-eye co-ordination and it will also engage your little one with animals and nature.**

Two little blackbirds, sitting on the wall
One named Peter, one named Paul
Fly away Peter, fly away Paul
Come back Peter, come back Paul

# Nursery rhymes

Nursery rhymes are a delightful way to enrich your child's development on many levels. The stories they contain, as well as the fascinating stories behind them, create vivid images that stimulate children's imagination. Most of us will remember at least a few nursery rhymes from our childhood and have memories of being comforted or entertained by their rhythm and language.

The tradition of passing on nursery rhymes orally has declined noticeably during the past decades, with fewer and fewer long-established stories, songs and rhymes being handed down through the generations. I firmly believe that these have an important place in our children's lives, not just because they keep our culture alive, but also because they are so rich in history, aid learning and teach good morals and behaviour. Plus they're age appropriate as well as just being plain good fun!

Most of the nursery rhymes that have been passed down have a strong, memorable rhythm, which helps to enrich children's vocabulary and speech development, and, when read with an adult, encourages early reading. Rhymes set to music inspire an early interest in song and harmony. Although the words of many seem to make little sense, some nursery rhymes introduce classic literature to children at an early age, not to mention a host of different topics that can be discussed. Learning rhymes also encourages the creative use of words and basic language skills. We've had great fun making up our own silly rhymes in our house, and I'm sure that part of this has to do with our love of nursery rhymes.

# OLD MACDONALD HAD A FARM

**Slot in the sounds of any familiar farm animals and sing with gusto! This song can go on forever, making it a perfect distraction for long car journeys.**

Old MacDonald had a farm
Ee-i-ee-i-oh!
And on that farm he had
some chickens
Ee-i-ee-i-oh!
With a cluck-cluck here
And a cluck-cluck there
Here a cluck, there a cluck
Everywhere a cluck-cluck
Old MacDonald had a farm
Ee-i-ee-i-oh!

Old MacDonald had a farm
Ee-i-ee-i-oh!
And on that farm he had some dogs
Ee-i-ee-i-oh!
With a woof-woof here

And a woof-woof there
Here a woof, there a woof
Everywhere a woof-woof
Old MacDonald had a farm
Ee-i-ee-i-oh!

Old MacDonald had a farm
Ee-i-ee-i-oh!
And on that farm he had
some turkeys
Ee-i-ee-i-oh!
With a gobble-gobble here
And a gobble-gobble there
Here a gobble, there a gobble
Everywhere a gobble-gobble
Old MacDonald had a farm
Ee-i-ee-i-oh!

There are too many to list, but here are some more traditonal nursery rhymes:

- This Little Piggy Went to Market
- Three Blind Mice
- London's Burning
- Hickory Dickory Dock
- Baa Baa Black Sheep
- Ding Dong Bell
- Georgie Porgie
- Hot Cross Buns
- Humpty Dumpty
- Ladybird, Ladybird
- Little Bo-Peep
- Mary Had a Little Lamb
- Jack and Jill
- Mary, Mary, Quite Contrary

# ARTS and CRAFTS

Sometimes, I walk into my kitchen and, in the words of a friend, it looks like "Widow Twankey's boudoir"! Feathers, glitter, ribbons, more glitter, more feathers, and a psychedelic snowstorm of sequins dazzle and shimmer everywhere. Try as I might to contain the arts and crafts area to the dining table, the mess manages to take over the house. I don't mind, as I don't want to impose too many restrictions on the girls' play and experiments, or their imaginations, but I do find myself fighting a losing battle against the chaos that ensues!

I have a drawer set aside for cotton wool, paper, colouring pens and pencils, paint and paintbrushes, sticky tape, glitter, glitter glue and craft glue, buttons, aluminium foil, stickers, googly eyes, string, yarn and all the other paraphernalia that inevitably accompany arts and crafts. I want my girls to be able to help themselves and choose what they want to make when the artistic impulse strikes, rather than always have to wait for me to find them. Spontaneous creativity is my mantra. There's only one rule: no glue on the carpet!

I love drawing with my children and we often sit down to make treasure maps, decorate boxes for our pirate booty (hoards of buttons) or make fairy houses. I also ensure that whatever we draw or make is posted on the fridge or the kitchen wall (if possible), so they know how much importance I place on their achievements and how much I value their work and their efforts. If not, it goes into my "Memory Box".

I remember watching the TV programme *Blue Peter* as a kid and feeling overwhelmingly frustrated by the fact that I did not have an endless supply of empty cartons and cereal boxes. As a result, I like to keep lots of supplies and an overflowing recycling bin that little hands can explore. My girls are endlessly enterprising, making extraordinary projects of their own devising with whatever they can find around the home. Ava's latest show-and-tell was a battleship she made with her Granddad out of a toothpaste box, a loo roll and some sticks!

Myleene
x

# ICE LANTERN

Turn your winter garden into a festival of light with these striking outdoor lanterns.

## WHAT YOU'LL NEED:

- **Small mixing bowl**
- **Cold water**
- **3 drops food colouring (optional)**
- **Toilet roll insert**
- **Small candle or tealight**

## WHAT TO DO:

Fill the bowl with water and mix in the food colouring if you would like the lantern to be coloured. Place the bowl in the freezer. After two hours, remove it and place the toilet roll insert in the centre of the bowl, pushing it down into the semi-frozen water by around 8cm. Return the bowl to the freezer for another 4 hours or so. Don't allow it to freeze completely as you must now remove the insert.

Return the bowl to the freezer for another 12 hours, or until it's frozen solid. Then put the candle or tea light in the hole, light it carefully and place it outside. The lantern base will last for days when the weather is sufficiently cold. This was introduced to me by Karen and I think it's absolutely genius. Truly magical!

# PASTA PICASSO

Teach your little one about shapes and patterns while you create imaginative artwork together. This is one time that playing with food is definitely OK.

## WHAT YOU'LL NEED:
- 200g dry spaghetti
- Kitchen roll
- Felt-tip pens
- Sheet of coloured paper
- Glue stick or craft glue

## WHAT TO DO:
Cook the spaghetti according to the instructions on the packet, drain, cool and pat dry with kitchen roll. Leftover spaghetti (without sauce) is also fine to use.

Ask your child to draw shapes, pictures or patterns on the coloured paper – swirls, circles, squares, wavy lines . . . whatever they like. Now, trace over the shapes and pictures with a line of glue. Press the pieces of cooked spaghetti onto the glue and leave to dry. How about a self-portrait or a pasta picture of mum and dad? Spaghetti is perfect for hair and the features can be added with a felt-tip pen. Once the glue has dried, display the artwork with pride!

# HOORAY SUNRAY

These colourful suncatchers are a great way to recycle the plastic lids from food packaging, and they couldn't be easier to make.

## WHAT YOU'LL NEED:
- **Plastic packaging lids**
- **Permanent marker pens (black and coloured)**
- **Hole punch**
- **Thread or ribbon**

## WHAT TO DO:
Make sure the plastic lids are clean and soak them to remove any sticky labels. Once dry, using a black marker pen, draw shapes or pictures on the lids and then colour them in, making them as cheerful and bright as possible. If your little one hasn't mastered the art of colouring in yet, encourage them to create a picture in their own way. The more colourful, the better.

Punch a hole in the centre of the top of the lid, thread through some ribbon and hang the suncatcher in front of a window where it will catch the light. String a few together to make a pretty mobile, or group several to make a seasonal display.

# CARDBOARD TUBE SKITTLES

Keep children occupied for hours, first making and then playing with these skittles. You can use this activity to practise basic numeracy skills too.

## WHAT YOU'LL NEED:
- **10 cardboard tubes (toilet roll or kitchen roll tubes are perfect)**
- **Coloured paper, paints and brush, felt-tip pens**
- **Craft glue**
- **Soft ball**

## WHAT TO DO:
Decorate the cardboard tubes and make them into characters. Toy soldiers are an obvious choice, but what about robots, superheroes, dolls or cats? If you don't have enough tubes to make a set in one go, make it a work-in-progress project and collect and decorate them over a few weeks. When the skittles set is complete, number them from one to ten in large, bold figures and take it in turns to see how many you can knock down in one go.

Sneak in a little simple maths practice. It can be as easy as counting the skittles as they are set up, or call out the numbers on the skittles as they are knocked down; or try to knock down odd or even numbers only; or practise subtraction and work out how many are still standing – we had ten, we knocked down four, so that leaves . . . ?

# SPONGE ART

Make wrapping paper, cards and pretty pictures using just a few old sponges and some coloured paint.

## WHAT YOU'LL NEED:

- **Several sponges (budget cleaning sponges with an abrasive back are fine, thin ones cut more easily)**
- **Scissors**
- **Poster paints**
- **Paper plates**
- **Sheet of plain and coloured paper**

## WHAT TO DO:

Help your child to cut out different shapes from the sponges. Squares, hearts and bows are great for wrapping paper designs, or choose something seasonal, like an Easter bunny or a Christmas bell. Fruit and vegetable shapes, flowers and animals are also fun, or circles on which faces and hair can be drawn. Anything you like!

Press out the sponge shapes. Pour out quantities of two or three colours of paint, one colour per plate. Press a shape into the paint (abrasive side up), making sure it is covered evenly, and carefully apply it to the card or paper. Rinse out the sponges between colours, or try blending two or three colours together to make different shades or effects. This is a great opportunity to show how red and yellow make orange, for example.

# 26

# EDIBLE ART

This is the perfect way for very young children to really experiment with finger painting. If most of what goes onto their hands ends up in their mouths, you can be confident that with this paint they won't be poisoned in the artistic process, even if they do get a sugar "high".

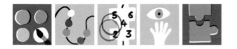

## WHAT YOU'LL NEED:
- Jelly cubes or powder, in different flavours
- Sheet of plain paper

## WHAT TO DO:
Mix the jelly according to the instructions on the packet, using half of the suggested amount of liquid (i.e. milk or water) to make the consistency a bit thicker. Place in the refrigerator for about fifteen minutes, or until it has set slightly. Prepare a few different flavours of jelly for a good selection of colours – you can always eat what you don't use!

Now, encourage your child to dip in their fingers and start painting! Shapes, swirls, flowers, anything they like. Best of all, hands can be licked clean between paintings and you may find you have very little mess to clear up!

# FELT CROWN

Be a prince or princess for the day. These felt crowns are easy to make and children can use their imagination making their own decorations.

## WHAT YOU'LL NEED:

- Large sheet of flexible card
- Scissors
- 2-3 felt squares in a single colour (adhesive-backed)
- Craft glue
- Decorations such as gems, felt or fabric pieces, feathers, large buttons, glitter, foil, coloured wool, pipe cleaners

## WHAT TO DO:

Make a crown template. On a large sheet of card, draw the shape of a crown - a traditional pointy one is fine - or use your imagination with your child's help to create something more elaborate, like a tiara with bobbles and swirls around the edges. Bend the card round your child's head to make sure it fits, and add an extra 2-3cm to one side edge for an overlap. Cut out the template, including the overlap. Place the template flat on a work surface. Remove the backing from the felt squares and place them over the crown, making sure that the whole of the

template is covered, except the overlap, and that the join between squares is neat. If you are not using adhesive-backed felt, glue on the felt squares and allow them to dry. Cut away the surplus felt from around the template. Bend the crown into a circle and, using the overlap, glue the sides together or stick them together with extra pieces of felt. Make sure the crown is completely dry and secure before decorating starts.

Decorate the crown with scrunched-up bits of foil; make patterns with sequins, glitter and buttons; glue on lengths of wool or ribbon to make stripes; cut out and stick on shapes from different coloured felt or other fabrics; bend pipe cleaners into hearts or jewel shapes - whatever looks the most regal. Now it's time to crown your little prince or princess.

# FANCY FAN

Keep cool during the hot summer months or complete
a Spanish señorita look with this decorative fan.

## WHAT YOU'LL NEED:

- **Strips of lace or pieces of coloured ribbon**
- **Large, square sheet of coloured paper**
- **Scissors**
- **Glitter, sequins or other decorations**
- **Paint and brush**
- **Craft glue**
- **Sticky tape**
- **Ribbon, to tie the base**

## WHAT TO DO:

Glue two or three strips of lace or ribbon across the top of the square on one side of the paper. Decorate the central part of the paper with sequins and glitter, or paint a picture. Once dry, fold the decorated paper back and forth into accordion creases 2cm in width.

Tape the undecorated base of the fan closed, and tie it with ribbon about 4cm from the end. Open out the top of the paper to create your fancy fan.

# PUZZLE PICTURES

This is a simple activity that can be adapted for children of all ages. Make the puzzle pieces large and square for very young children, while smaller and more intricate shapes will be suitable for older children.

## WHAT YOU'LL NEED:

- **Large picture cut from a magazine or newspaper, or downloaded from the Internet (or download a colouring sheet for your child to fill in)**
- **Sheet of thick card, same size as the picture**
- **Craft glue**
- **Thick felt-tip pen**
- **Scissors**

## WHAT TO DO:

Glue the picture or your child's artwork onto the card and allow it to dry. Mark out the puzzle pieces with the felt-tip pen and cut them out. Four large, chunky pieces are probably enough for a two-year-old, while eight or more pieces will keep an older child occupied.

Jumble the pieces up and ask your child to put the picture back together again. Puzzle pictures make a great activity gift for Granny or Granddad, that they can then help your child put together.

# DEAR SANTA

Post letters to Father Christmas, the Easter bunny or a favourite soft toy in this easy-to-make postbox. It's also great for playing post office!

## WHAT YOU'LL NEED:

- **Empty tissue box**
- **Poster paints and brush**
- **Stickers, glitter, buttons, etc.**
- **Craft glue**

## WHAT TO DO:

Paint the top and sides of the tissue box, leaving the hole in the top open - who says a postbox has to be red! Once it is dry, decorate it with stickers, glitter, buttons, etc.

Why not write your child's initial in buttons or sequins on the front and add "R" beside it for an authentic British postbox touch. If it's to be used at Christmas, glue a layer of cotton wool to the top for a snowy effect.

# LET IT SNOW

The glittery scenes inside snow shakers or snow globes fascinate young children. Create a wintry scene around something that interests your child, using a tiny toy car or a fairy figure, or even a character from a favourite TV show. If you don't have a spare plastic figure, try making your own from modelling clay.

## WHAT YOU'LL NEED:

- **Empty jam jar with watertight lid**
- **Water, boiled previously and cooled**
- **2 tsp glycerine**
- **1 tsp washing-up liquid**
- **5-6 tbsp glitter (silver or white make good snow scenes, coloured glitter is also pretty)**
- **Small plastic figure (or one made out of modelling clay)**
- **Waterproof glue**

## WHAT TO DO:

Fill the jam jar with the water to about 1cm from the top. Add the glycerine and washing-up liquid and stir to combine. Add the glitter and put the jar to one side. Glue the figure or toy to the centre of the inside of the lid. When it's dry, carefully insert the figure down into the jar and screw on the lid. Make sure it's screwed on tightly, turn the jar upside down, shake and let it snow!

# EGG CARTON BUGS

Use a row of egg carton cups to create a caterpillar or single cups to make butterflies and other colourful insects. When finished the bugs can be hung from a coat hanger to make an instant mobile.

## WHAT YOU'LL NEED:

- **Empty egg cartons**
- **Scissors**
- **Poster paints and brush**
- **Craft glue**
- **Tissue paper, googly eyes, black pipe cleaners, bits of felt, glitter. Anything to make your insects come to life!**
- **Elastic strings**

## WHAT TO DO:

To make a caterpillar, remove the lids from the cartons and cut the bottoms into halves, lengthways. Paint the outside of each cup a different colour and allow to dry. Use the first cup in a row to make the head. Attach the eyes with glue, then poke two holes in the top of the cup and insert pipe cleaners for antennae. Pipe-cleaner legs can be inserted through holes in the sides of the remaining carton cups. Create a pair of legs by threading one pipe cleaner through two holes aligned on opposite sides of a cup. Line up several rows of cups for a lovely long caterpillar.

Or why not make a butterfly? Make tissue-paper wings and sprinkle them with glitter before gluing them onto the top of a carton cup. Add eyes, antennae and legs as for the caterpillar and paint, draw or stick on decorations to make your butterfly as colourful as possible.

# NO-MESS FINGERPAINT PAD

This is the perfect way to keep a creative child busy, with no mess. Make sure they don't use their fingernails, or this mess-free activity will spring a leak.

## WHAT YOU'LL NEED:
- **Large zip-seal bag**
- **Thick paint, such as Tempera, in several colours**
- **Masking tape**

## WHAT TO DO:
Squeeze blobs of different colours of paint into the bag. Place it on a flat surface and press out the air. Zip the bag shut and secure it to the top of a wipe-clean work surface with masking tape. Point the opening away from the child in case of leaks.

Now, encourage your child to squish the paint around the bag in all directions with their fingers, to make a colourful picture. Or why not ask them to make patterns, draw shapes or write their name in the swirl of paint? You can create hours of mess-free fun, as well as the opportunity to teach your child a little bit about primary and secondary colours.

# SCRAPBOOK COLLAGES

Most children love creating collages and you are probably used to finding examples of your little one's creative impulses around the house. Collect them in a collage scrapbook and you'll have an ongoing record of their artistic development.

## WHAT YOU'LL NEED:

- **Sturdy scrapbook with thick paper pages**
- **Scraps of fabric, felt, aluminium foil, garden leaves or pressed flowers (see page 111) buttons, glitter, haberdashery items such as ribbon and ric rac, pictures from magazines or newspapers – or even family photos**
- **Scissors**
- **Craft glue**
- **Paints and brush**

## WHAT TO DO:

Help your child to cut out different shapes or patterns from fabric or paper and glue them onto a page of the scrapbook. Cut out pictures from magazines or use pressed leaves or flowers from the garden. Choose a theme, such as "winter", "flowers" or "farmyard animals", and see what you can find around the house to create an attractive collage. Paint the back of your shapes and glue them on. Leave the scrapbook open to dry – you can come back to it on another day if you would like to add more.

Use collage techniques for other crafts too. I recently spent an afternoon at Ava's school talking about fashion design. We created collage-style moodboards which the girls loved making, with scraps of fabric, magazine pictures and their own drawings.

# COLOUR COLLAGES

Use scraps of paper cut from magazines as your medium for this project and create a colour-themed picture or design.

## WHAT YOU'LL NEED:
- Old magazines
- Children's scissors
- Craft glue
- Sheet of plain or coloured paper, or card

## WHAT TO DO:
Sit down with your child and look through some old magazines for examples of their favourite colour. If they have mastered using scissors, they may be able to cut out whole images, such as a red shirt, shoes, lipstick or a nice red apple – whatever you can find in their favourite colour. Or ask them just to cut out areas of the colour in circles, squares and strips.

Once you have a pile of shapes or images, you can begin making the collage. Glue them in an abstract pattern on the paper or card, or draw a picture or a shape to fill in with the colour. There's no need to be restricted to just one colour of course, make a multi-coloured pattern or build up different colours to form a rainbow.

Another fun idea is to cut from squares of paper in a variety of different colours to create a colourful mosaic. Older children may enjoy drawing a picture first, and then filling it with coloured squares. Little ones may simply wish to "create". Mosaics are a fantastic way to improve spatial awareness.

# BIG BOX TRAIN

Let your little one be a train driver for the day. This is a great activity if you have more than one child in tow.

## WHAT YOU'LL NEED:

- **Large box, one per child (large enough for your child to stand in)**
- **Sticky tape**
- **Scissors**
- **Paper plates**
- **Craft glue**
- **Empty plastic drinks bottle, washed**
- **Poster paints and brush**
- **Length of wide ribbon, for two shoulder straps**

## WHAT TO DO:

Tape the box shut and cut off the top. Turn it over and cut a square opening in the bottom of the box, closer to one end than the other. When your child stands inside the opening, there should be a piece of box at the front, wide enough to support the smokestack, and a smaller piece at the back. Glue paper plates onto the sides of the box for wheels. Create a small hole in the top of the box at the front of the train. Insert the drinks bottle neck (minus the cap) into the hole and push/screw it down. Secure with tape on the inside of the box if necessary.

To finish, paint windows on the sides for a passenger train, or some coal or bricks for a freight train. Don't forget to paint the wheels and some lights at the front. When the paint has dried, punch two small holes just below the opening on either side of the top of the train, one at the front and one at the back. Cut the ribbon into two equal lengths and thread the ends through the holes, one ribbon on each side of the train, and knot the ends to secure them. When your child steps inside the train, the ribbons will act as carrying straps over the shoulders.

# GIANT TISSUE PAPER FLOWERS

These lovely flowers are unbelievably easy to make, even for tiny hands, and can be attached to pipe-cleaner stems to create a floral display or make attractive gifts.

## WHAT YOU'LL NEED:

- **6-8 large sheets of tissue paper of any colour, plus 2 sheets of green for leaves**
- Scissors
- Twist-ties and pipe cleaners

## WHAT TO DO:

Stack all the sheets of tissue paper in a pile, one on top of the other. Make sure the edges are lined up and then cut the sheets in half. Place one of the smaller piles on top of the other. Ideally, you should now have about 12 to 16 sheets. Starting at one end, fold *all* the layers of tissue paper back and forth into 2cm accordion pleats. When you have finished the whole pile, use a twist tie or a pipe cleaner to tie the pleated tissue paper in the centre. Fold any leftover wire downwards and attach another pipe cleaner to form a stem.

Using the scissors, trim both ends of the tissue paper layers into a half circle, or cut them to a point, to make the petals look realistic when opened out. Carefully separate the layers of tissue paper and, one by one, pull them gently upwards from the centre to form the petals. Your giant flower has just blossomed. To create leaves, simply add two layers of green tissue paper to the bottom of the pile of coloured tissue, and trim them into a leaf shape. This will make a perfect gift for Mother's day from your child.

# TISSUE PAPER BOWLS

These beautiful, translucent bowls are easy to make from colourful papier-mâché. Make them in a single colour or a whole rainbow of colours to form pretty gifts or to store something special.

## WHAT YOU'LL NEED:
- **Coloured tissue paper (4-5 large sheets for a medium-sized bowl)**
- **White craft glue and water**
- **Jam jar**
- **Brush, for glue**
- **Plastic bowl (the size you want your finished bowl to be)**
- **Cling film**

## WHAT TO DO:
Tear the tissue paper into strips of around 2 x 10cm. Add equal amounts of glue and water to the jam jar and shake or stir to mix well. Cover the back of the bowl with two layers of cling film. Smooth it down to eliminate creases and leave a small amount protruding above the edge of the bowl. Tuck the spare cling film inside the bowl and place it upside down on some newspaper, on a flat surface. Coat the whole surface of the bowl with the water-glue solution, and carefully paste on strips of tissue paper, making sure that the whole bowl is covered. For a neat edge, paste long strips of tissue paper around the circumference (or trim the edge with scissors when the finished bowl is dry). Add another coat of glue and repeat the process.

Carry on building up the layers until the bowl is thick and sturdy. You'll need at least five or six layers, taking care to keep them of an even thickness overall, apart from the base which can be built up a little for stability. Set it to one side. Take hold of the extra cling film at the top edge and carefully remove the plastic bowl and cling film. Leave the bowl for a few more hours to dry out completely.

# FELT BOOKMARKS

Keep track of your place in a bedtime storybook or make this bookmark as a gift. The trick is to use flattish decorations so that the bookmark will slip neatly between the pages.

## WHAT YOU'LL NEED:

- **Felt, in several different colours**
- **Scissors**
- **Sequins, glitter, sticky paper shapes, small feathers, thin craft foam, etc.**
- **Craft glue**

## WHAT TO DO:

Cut out a strip of felt about 4cm wide and 18cm long. Create a fringe by cutting thin strips into one end of the felt. Decorate the rest of the bookmark with shapes cut out from different coloured pieces of felt or craft foam.

You need decorations that will lie flat and not make the bookmark too bulky. "Write" your child's initial in sequins or glitter, or, if it's to be a gift, spell out the name of the recipient. This bookmark won't work with an e-reader, but you can certainly use it in this book!

# PLAY CLAY

All kids love to knead, squeeze and roll out squidgy stuff, and this easy-to-make clay is not only inexpensive, it's harmless if eaten. The clay shapes can be painted once dry, or coloured with food colouring.

## WHAT YOU'LL NEED:

- **Large bowl**
- **1 mug oatmeal (fine oats are best)**
- **½ mug plain flour, plus extra for dusting**
- **¼ mug water**
- **Food colouring (optional)**
- **Rolling pin and cookie cutters**
- **Poster paints and brush (optional)**

## WHAT TO DO:

Combine the oatmeal, flour and water in a large bowl and mix them together, including the food colouring if required. Add a little more flour if the clay is too sticky, and a little more water if too dry. Turn the clay out onto a floured surface and knead it for three or four minutes, until it is firm yet pliant. If you don't want to use it right away it can be stored in an airtight container for up to two weeks.

Children can mould the clay into their own artistic creations with their hands, or roll it out pastry-style and use cookie cutters to create different shapes. Place the clay shapes and figures on greaseproof paper on a tray and leave in a warm place overnight to dry out. Make sure you allow the clay to dry out completely if you intend to paint it.

# PLAY DOUGH

This dough will last for weeks in an airtight container, but it's not the edible kind. It can be used plain, but adding colour makes it more fun and your little one can create everything from worms and monsters to fairies and animals, or even plates of "food".

## WHAT YOU'LL NEED:
- ½ mug fine salt
- 1 mug plain flour, plus extra for dusting
- 1 tbsp cream of tartar
- 1 tbsp vegetable oil
- 1 mug boiling water
- Glitter (optional)
- Food colouring (optional)

## WHAT TO DO:
Combine all the dry ingredients in a bowl and stir well. Sprinkle in some glitter if you're making something sparkly like stars or fairies. If using food colouring, add 4-5 drops to the mug of boiling water. Add the vegetable oil and boiling water to the dry ingredients and stir vigorously until well combined and cool enough to touch. Knead the dough with your hands on a floured surface and roll it into a ball.

Once it's cool your child can get to work modelling or making shapes and figures, or it can be stored in an airtight container if you don't want to use it straightaway. The quantities can be reduced if you want to make smaller amounts of several different colours of dough.

# COMB PAINTING

This is an inventive way of creating a textured, patterned picture. If you don't have an old comb, make one out of a piece of stiff cardboard.

## WHAT YOU'LL NEED:
- **4 tbsp plain flour**
- **4 tbsp water**
- **Bowl for mixing**
- **Paint in one or a variety of colours**
- **Palette knife**
- **White or coloured paper, or card**
- **Comb**

## WHAT TO DO:
Mix the flour and water together in a bowl until you have a smooth paste. Stir in a little paint to add colour. If you want to use a number of different colours, divide the plain paste into individual pots and colour each separately. Spread the paste across the paper with a palette knife. Now drag the teeth of the comb down through the paste and across the paper to produce patterns. The paste will dry leaving a textured effect.

Show your child how to create different patterns by dragging the comb this way and that, criss-crossing lines and building up areas with more paste.

# FOIL ART

Children love the pliability and texture of foil - a kitchen cupboard staple - not to mention its shiny surface. Here are some suggestions for ways to use it.

- **FOIL ETCHING:** Fold a sheet of foil in half (to make it thicker) and "draw" pictures on it with a lolly stick or an unsharpened pencil.

- **FOIL PAINTING:** Using poster paints, paint a colourful picture on a sheet of foil. Make use of its shiny surface and leave areas blank to form a pond or stream, or the windows of a house.

- **FOIL JEWELLERY:** Scrunch foil into little balls and glue them onto ribbons to create beautiful necklaces and bracelets.

- **FOIL PICTURE:** Glue lengths of wool or string onto a piece of cardboard to create a picture or design. Cut out a sheet of foil 4–5cm larger than the cardboard, place it over the picture and press it down carefully over the wool or string to make a textured foil picture. Wrap the excess foil neatly around the edge of the cardboard to hold it in place.

- **FOIL PICTURE FRAMES:** Cut out a frame template from a large piece of cardboard, brush it with glue and wrap foil around it. The foil doesn't need to lie flat; in fact, raised bumps and lumps will add authenticity to the "old master" look. Glue on foil shapes or scrunched-up foil balls to create patterns and textures.

- **FOIL SAILBOAT:** Cover a small box with foil to make it watertight. Press a small ball of modelling clay to the bottom of the inside of the box and insert a lolly stick or straw into it as a mast. Cut out a triangle of white paper, punch a hole in the top and bottom, and slip it over the mast to make a sail. Good for simple bath-time fun.

# 44

# FOIL ROBOT

This robot is a perfect project for a rainy day. If you don't have a cardboard tube to hand, an empty tissue box will do. The foil adds an authentic metal finish.

## WHAT YOU'LL NEED:

- Cardboard tube (toilet roll or kitchen roll tubes are perfect)
- Aluminium foil
- Craft glue and brush
- Googly eyes, or a pen to draw them
- Coloured craft paper, sequins, buttons
- Silver pipe cleaners

## WHAT TO DO:

Cut out a sheet of aluminium foil large enough to cover the whole tube. Coat the back of the foil with glue and stick it onto the tube, carefully tucking the excess down into the tube ends.

Stick on googly eyes, or draw eyes on paper circles, and paste them in position. Next, small pieces of foil, craft paper shapes, sequins or plastic buttons, make a tiny control panel and glue it to the robot's chest. Poke two small holes through either side of the robot's head, and thread a pipe cleaner through each, twisting it around to create curly antennae.

# PAPER DOLLS OR SUPERHEROES

Most of us will have memories of making paper dolls at some point in our childhood, but you don't need to stick at dolls, you can use the same technique to make chains of paper superheroes, animals or flowers too.

## WHAT YOU'LL NEED:
- **Sheets of thick white or coloured paper**
- **Felt-tip pens and/or paints and brush**
- **Scissors**
- **Scraps of fabric, wool, sequins, buttons, googly eyes, yarn or felt to decorate**
- **Craft glue**

## WHAT TO DO:
Fold a sheet of paper back and forth into accordion pleats 5–7cm in width. On the top pleat draw a doll, superhero or any other figure, making sure that part of it (such as the arms) fills the entire width of the pleat. This part will not be cut out entirely so that when unfolded the figures will be joined together. Holding the pleated paper tightly shut, carefully cut out around the figure with scissors.

Unfold the paper to produce a chain of identical, linking figures. Draw or paint their faces and use wool for hair, or paste on googly eyes. Draw or paint clothing and decorate the bodies with bits of fabric and glitter, or whatever you have to hand. There's no limit to the figures you can make, from ballerinas and fairies, to farmers and postmen, princes and princesses, and superheroes, or anything else that takes your little one's fancy. Tape several chains together to create a jolly frieze for the playroom or kitchen, or for seasonal celebrations.

# 46

# PASTA NECKLACE

You are bound to have the material for this necklace in your kitchen cupboard. It's a fun way of encouraging creativity and hand-eye co-ordination.

## WHAT YOU'LL NEED:
- **Dry pasta shapes with holes through the centre (e.g., rigatoni or penne, large shapes are best for the littlest hands)**
- **Poster paints and brush**
- **White craft glue, glitter (optional)**
- **Thick cord, string or ribbon**
- **Sticky tape**

## WHAT TO DO:
Lay the pasta shapes out on some newspaper, paint them in a variety of colours and allow to dry. For a shiny effect, stir a little white craft glue into the paint, or sprinkle glitter onto the pasta while the paint is still wet. Cut a necklace-length piece of cord or string (long enough to fit over your little one's head – or yours, if it will be a gift!), and wrap a little sticky tape around one end to create a hard point, rather like a needle.

Thread the cord through one of the pasta shapes, and tie a knot large enough at the other end to stop the pasta falling off, or tie the string around a spent matchstick to act as a temporary stop. Continue to thread more shapes onto the string until you have finished the necklace, and secure with a knot. Cut off any excess string and the necklace is ready to wear.

# MIRROR IMAGE ART

Children can use the mirror image technique to create pictures that are magically identical. Subjects that work well include butterflies, faces and flowers or any kind of pattern.

## WHAT YOU'LL NEED:
- **Sheets of coloured or white paper**
- **Paint in a variety of colours**
- **Paintbrushes**

## WHAT TO DO:
Fold a piece of paper in half to create a crease down the centre. Open it out and lay it flat on the table. Ask your child to paint a design or half a picture on one side of the paper only, making sure they use enough paint for the image to transfer. Use several different colours and a fresh brush for each colour, or rinse and dry carefully between them.

While the paint is still wet (important), carefully fold the paper along the crease and press down so that the paint is transferred from one side of the paper to the other. Open it out slowly to reveal what your little one has created.

# 48

# WOOL PICTURES

One way to use scraps of leftover wool is to create a textured picture. With a little imagination, you'll find that wool can be very versatile.

## WHAT YOU'LL NEED:

- **Sheet of plain, coloured paper or card, or aluminium foil**
- **Craft glue and brush**
- **Pieces of coloured wool**
- **Scissors**

## WHAT TO DO:

Using the brush, draw a picture or pattern on the paper, card or foil with glue. If your little one likes to take their time and you are worried about the glue drying, sketch the design first in pencil and then follow the outline in glue, a little at a time. Attach pieces of wool to the glue to create a textured artwork, using different colours to create a jazzy effect.

Wind a piece of wool round and round to make a wheel for a car, cut a piece of yellow wool into strips for a thatched roof, make a poodle on a leash. Small pom poms are perfect for this (see page 87) or for puffs of smoke coming out of a chimney.

# BLOWING EGGS

Eggs are not just for Easter, it's great fun to decorate them at any time of year. Young children will need help with this activity since needles are involved and you need a lot of puff to blow the fragile eggs.

## WHAT YOU'LL NEED:

- Several eggs, washed and dried
- A large needle
- 2 bowls, 1 large
- 30ml kitchen bleach
- Poster paints and brush, for decorating
- Kitchen roll

## WHAT TO DO:

Hold an egg gently in one hand and very carefully pierce a hole in one end with the darning needle. You may need to start the hole with a finer needle and then widen it with the darning needle, gently pushing and rotating it in the hole. Turn the egg over and make a hole at the other end. Widen the second hole so that it's bigger than the first. Push the needle deep into the egg (through the wider hole) to break the yolk, and carefully stir the contents around inside the egg with the needle to help them come out more easily.

Hold the egg over the smaller bowl, place your mouth to the small hole and blow as hard as you can to push out all the contents. If you don't want to use your mouth, you can use an oral syringe, the type with a large opening (no needle) that is used for children's medicine. Repeat with the other eggs.

Pour the bleach into a large bowl and fill it to the top with water. Submerge the eggs in this solution for thirty minutes to sterilise them, then remove, rinse and dry them. Leave the eggs on some kitchen roll to dry overnight and then they are ready to decorate with paint or dye.

Using poster paints, show your child how to create different patterns, shapes and designs on their eggs.

# 50

# POM POMS

A fun way of using up leftover wool, pom poms are so easy to make. You can combine them to create all sorts of pom-pom pals, or flowers and decorations.

## WHAT YOU'LL NEED:

- Cardboard
- Scissors
- Wool
- Googly eyes and bits of felt to decorate
- Craft glue
- Pipe cleaners, for flower stems, insect legs, etc.

WHAT TO DO.

Choose something round as a template, such as the base of a glass, and draw two circles of the same size on the cardboard. A diameter of around 5cm is perfect for a small pom pom. Draw another circle about 2cm in diameter (a 1p coin is about the right size) in the centre of the large ones. Cut out the large circles, then the small circles in the middle and place the two doughnut-shaped templates together.

Wind the wool around the template, feeding it through the hole, then across the front of the template, around the back and out through the hole again. Continue wrapping the wool around the template until all of it is covered and or all the wool is used up. Carry on wrapping with a fresh piece of wool, changing colour if you like, until you have built up a nice thick doughnut.

At the outer edge of the doughnut, push the point of the scissors through the wool layers and between the two templates, and begin cutting. You'll probably find it easiest to cut a few layers at a time. Make sure you hold the template securely so that the cut wool remains in place. When you've cut through all the layers, right around the edge of the doughnut, pass a length of wool between the two pieces of cardboard. Wiggle it down, pull it tight and tie it firmly at the centre. Ease off the templates and trim off any long pieces of wool. Your pom pom is ready for action.

 **ARTS AND CRAFTS** 87

# STORE CUPBOARD ART

Raid the kitchen store cupboard for the materials to create an imaginative textured picture out of dried pasta and rice.

## WHAT YOU'LL NEED:

- **Sheet of thick coloured paper or white card**
- **Pencil**
- **Craft glue**
- **Paper plate**
- **Dry pasta shapes, uncooked rice**
- **Poster paints and brush**

## WHAT TO DO:

Ask your child to draw a design or the outline of a simple picture on the paper or card. Pour some glue onto a paper plate. Dip the pasta shapes in the glue and stick them onto the paper - they can just follow the outline of the design or picture, or you can fill in whole areas. Spread glue over the area to be filled in and attach pasta shapes or sprinkle rice over the glued area. The excess rice can be shaken off when dry, or patient little fingers can apply the grains carefully one by one.

Spaghetti makes great hair for pasta portraits. When the glue has dried, the pasta and rice can be painted to make a perfect pasta picture.

# NIGHT SKY MOBILE

Teach your little one about the moon and the stars when you make this simple mobile. Luminous (glow-in-the-dark) paint adds the perfect finishing touch for a darkened bedroom.

## WHAT YOU'LL NEED:

- Thick card or cardboard
- Felt-tip pen
- Scissors or craft knife
- White, silver, yellow, blue or luminous paint
- Paintbrush
- 2 wooden dowels or sticks
- Hole punch
- Wool or string

## WHAT TO DO:

Draw star and crescent moon shapes on the cardboard with a felt-tip pen and cut them out. You will need five shapes in total. Paint one side, allow the shapes to dry, then turn them over and paint the other side. Why not add a rocket, a spaceship, an astronaut or some planets? This is a great opportunity to teach children about space, the solar system and the order of the planets!

Place one dowel or stick over the other at right angles and, using the wool or string, tie them together at the centre in the shape of a cross. Punch a hole in the end of each shape and tie a piece of wool or string to each one, using a different length for each shape to vary the mobile, and then tie the shapes to the ends of the cross and one to the centre. Tie another piece of string to the centre of the cross and your mobile is now ready to hang.

If you don't have wooden dowels or sticks to make the mobile support, just hang your shapes from two coat hangers fixed together at right angles, or even just one coat hanger would do.

 ARTS AND CRAFTS 89

# MONSTER TISSUE BOXES

Frighten the whole family with these easy-to-make monsters.
They can be decorated with anything from buttons and
feathers to glitter and sequins, or try luminous paint for
scaring people in the dark.

## WHAT YOU'LL NEED:

- **Empty tissue box**
- **Empty egg carton**
- **Poster paints and brush**
- **Sequins, polka dots, feathers, large buttons, glitter, to decorate**
- **Craft glue**
- **White felt or craft foam**
- **Googly eyes**

## WHAT TO DO:

Paint the entire tissue box and two or three egg carton
cups. When dry, decorate the box with whatever you have
to hand – sequins, spots, feathers, or anything else to give
your monster a unique look, but leave the area around
the opening clear. While the glue on the decorations is
drying, draw two rows of jagged teeth on the white felt or
foam. They should be wide enough to fit the box opening.

Cut out the teeth and glue one set inside the box just
above the opening and the other just below it, so that the
two rows of teeth show through ferociously. Glue a googly
eye to the front of each egg carton cup to make horrible,
protruding eyeballs and glue them onto the monster
body. And don't forget that some monsters have just one
or even several eyes!

# YOGHURT POT FLOWERS

This is a great way to recycle yoghurt pots and create a beautiful floral display. Little ones may need some help with the cutting out.

## WHAT YOU'LL NEED:

- Several empty yoghurt pots, washed and dried
- Scissors
- Poster paint in several colours and brush
- Green straws (bendy ones are best)
- Craft glue

## WHAT TO DO:

Using the scissors, cut down the sides of the yoghurt pots to create wide strips that will form the petals, but don't cut into the base itself. Shape the tops of the petals by cutting them into semi-circles or points. Place the pots upside down on some newspaper and, using the tips of the scissors, pierce a hole in the centre of the base of each. Paint the pots in an array of beautiful colours.

When they are dry, insert a straw into each hole, threading it through so that the short part above the bendy bit protrudes above the base of the pot - this will form the flower stamens. Glue the straw in position. When dry, make the stamens by cutting thin strips lengthways down the short part of the straw. The long part becomes the stem. Now all that's left is to arrange your flowers in a pretty vase.

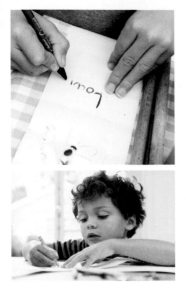

# MEMORY BOX

Collecting precious items in an imaginatively decorated box is a lovely way for children to keep a record of their achievements, interests and favourite things.

## WHAT YOU'LL NEED:
- Shoebox, or any box with a lid
- Poster paints and brush, adhesive backed stickers, glitter, feathers, large buttons, anything that will make your child's memory box unique
- Craft glue
- Googly eyes
- Scissors

## WHAT TO DO:
Begin by decorating the box and lid. You could tie the decoration in with your child's current interests, and paint a car or a favourite character on it. While it's drying help your child to think of what they might like to put in it. Look through family photos and choose two or three that are important to your child. Help them to cut out pictures of favourite toys and food from magazines or catalogues.

Pop in a few small toys or keepsakes. Take a print of your child's hand or foot, make a note of their height, weight and age, seal a lock of their hair in some cling film and don't forget examples of their artwork and shells or small stones from a trip to the beach – in fact, anything that provides a snapshot of your child at the age they are now.

Before you fill it, write your child's name and the date on the base of the box. You can add to it as time goes by or make a new box every year on their birthday. In years to come looking through the boxes will provide a nostalgic, heart-warming trip down memory lane.

# GREEN
# FINGERS

Gardening is a wonderful way of introducing children to the natural world, putting them in touch with nature and the multitude of insects, animals and plants that make every garden unique. Whatever space in your garden you can allocate to your child whether it is some empty planters, a tray of pots on a balcony or windowsill, or even their own small plot, you can undertake all sorts of gardening projects together and grow a variety of edible and non-edible plants.

Best of all, they'll learn to be responsible, and what happens when they're not! They'll also learn patience, as even the quickest-growing plants take a little time to become established. Yesterday, my friend told me that she had a present for me - a plant. I'm sure the utter horror and confusion on my face said it all, as she added hastily, "Don't worry, it's fully grown and I've given it six months' worth of plant food." The thing is, my house is a place where plants come to die. Try as I might, I just can't keep them alive. I have, however, tried to inspire my girls to grow plants, both indoors and out, if only just to illustrate how nature works. We grow the easy stuff - sunflowers, cress, chives, etc. The look of pure joy and satisfaction on Ava's face when she tells me proudly that all that came from one seed, is enough to keep me persevering.

My parents grow everything in their garden and the girls really enjoy seeing how the whole process fits together, from seed to table. They counted each one of the potatoes they dug up and were full of excitement telling me all about it, as we sat and ate our home-grown baked potatoes with cheese for lunch. Ava even kept the odd-shaped potatoes that looked like "birds", "a mountain" and "granddad" on her bedside table!

So, can I claim to be a model gardener? Sadly . . . no! Ultimately, whether you're blessed with green fingers or not, the key is inspiring your children to venture out into the garden and see how plants can be nurtured and grown and where some of the food on the table comes. At the very least, it gets you all outside!

Myleene
x

# Getting to grips with greenery

● Don't worry about the mess! Kids love getting dirty and working in the garden is a sensual way to experience nature. Keep a set of old clothes to hand that you don't mind getting grubby and dirty.

● For very little children, choose seeds that germinate quickly. Cress, herbs, salad leaves and radishes are great starter plants. You can also buy plug plants to give you a head start and keep interest levels high.

● Interest children by choosing plants they can use in food, such as herbs and fruit and vegetables.

● Choose easy-to-grow plants that are robust enough to succeed. Your local nursery will be able to offer some advice.

● Encourage experimentation. What happens if you pop just one seed in a hole and what happens if you plant twenty? Set aside special times when you can look after your plants together so you can offer gentle guidance about plant care; for example, it's as easy to over- as to under water

● Be prepared to stop a gardening session when your little one loses interest; the attention span of even the most attentive child will be shorter than yours.

● Invest in some child-sized tools. They are designed for small hands and with safety in mind. Blunt gardening scissors with a safety catch will allow your child to cut flowers and even do some basic pruning, without coming to harm.

# 56

# POTATO HEDGEHOG

Grown on a bright kitchen windowsill, this grass-topped potato friend will soon provide interesting results for impatient small gardeners.

## WHAT YOU'LL NEED:
- **Large baking potato (a flattish, oval potato works best)**
- **Paring knife**
- **Spoon and/or melon scoop**
- **Marker pen with a thick tip**
- **Cotton wool**
- **Small packet of grass seed**

## WHAT TO DO:
Draw a circle or an oval on the top of the potato, leaving about 4cm of uncut potato at one end for the head and a rim of around 1cm around the rest. Scoop out the top of the potato to form a hollow around 2cm deep. Little ones can use a spoon to scrape out any remaining uneven bits and then score the bottom and sides with a chunky child-friendly fork. Use a marker pen to draw the hedgehog's face, with a round nose and some whiskers. Fill the hollow with enough cotton wool to protrude just above the top of the potato, then soak it with water.

Sprinkle some grass seed on top of the wet cotton wool, covering the whole surface, and press it down gently. Place the hedgehog on a plate and stand it on a warm, light windowsill. The seeds should begin to germinate in just a few days and your hedgehog will start to grow a fine mane of green hair. Help your child to trim it into the latest salon style as it grows. Spray the hedgehog with water from time to time to keep the grass moist.

# CREATING A HERB GARDEN

Many herbs grow quickly, which makes them ideal plants for impatient young children, while you can enjoy experimenting with the different flavours in the kitchen. Herbs in pots also make welcome and useful gifts.

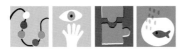

## WHAT YOU'LL NEED:
- **Large plant pot (or several smaller ones)**
- **Several stones, for drainage**
- **Garden compost**
- **Herb seeds (dill, parsley, chives, lavender, rosemary and mint all grow well)**
- **Watering can with a fine rose**
- **Cling film**

## WHAT TO DO:
Place a few stones in the bottom of the pot or container to assist drainage. Fill it with garden compost until it is about three-quarters full. Gently press a seed (or seeds) into the soil, cover with a fine layer of compost and press down gently. Using a watering can with a fine rose, water the pot until all the compost is moist, but not saturated.

Cover the top of the pot with cling film to retain warmth and moisture and place it in a sunny, warm position. Water regularly so that the compost does not dry out. When the seedlings start to emerge, remove the cling film. When they are 10–15cm in height, they can be transplanted to larger pots or to a garden bed. Regular cutting (for your culinary experiments) will help them continue to grow.

# GROWING TOMATOES

Strangely, many children dislike tomatoes and will only eat them if hidden away in a pasta sauce or a pizza topping. Freshly grown, sun-ripened tomatoes are not only much tastier than the traditional supermarket varieties, the whole process of growing them cannot fail to engage your little one. Perhaps it may even tempt them to try one!

## WHAT YOU'LL NEED:
- **Small plant pots**
- **Garden compost**
- **Tomato seeds**
- **Watering can with a fine rose**

## WHAT TO DO:
Start off the plants indoors. Fill the plant pots about three-quarters full with compost. Place three tomato seeds in each pot, spaced out evenly, and press them down lightly into the soil. Sprinkle more compost on top so that the seeds are covered and water using a fine rose so that the soil is moist but not saturated. Place the pots on a windowsill, or somewhere warm and sunny. Don't let the compost dry out and when the first seedlings start to appear, water them daily.

Once all risk of frost has passed and the plants are around 8cm in height, they can be transplanted into larger pots. Plant them singly in pots around 30cm wide, in fresh compost, or plant several in a grow bag. Water regularly and feed them every week with tomato plant food. They will need to be tied to stakes to keep them upright once they really start to grow.

# GROWING CRESS

Cress grows very quickly and is delicious eaten in sandwiches, salads, or on its own. Try using a variety of different cress seeds, to see which ones your child likes best.

## WHAT YOU'LL NEED:
- Empty egg carton or yoghurt pots, washed and dried
- Cotton wool
- Cress seeds

## WHAT TO DO:
Soak the cotton wool in water, and place it in the bottom of the egg carton cups or yoghurt pots. Use enough to fill about two-thirds of each cup or pot. Sprinkle the seeds over the cotton wool and gently press them down. Place the cups or pots in a bright, warm position, such as on a sunny windowsill. Keep the cotton wool moist, and watch the cress grow. The first cress should be ready to harvest a week or 10 days after planting.

# GROWING A PUMPKIN

Pumpkins are very satisfying to grow, not just to carve into jack-o'-lanterns at Halloween, as they can grow to mammoth proportions and retain your children's interest for months. Ava and Hero didn't want to carve their home-made pumpkin, so we drew faces on oranges with felt-tip pens instead!

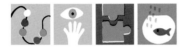

## WHAT YOU'LL NEED:

- **Several pumpkin seeds**
- **Small pot**
- **Handful of small stones**
- **Garden compost**
- **Watering can with a fine rose**
- **Napkin or piece of kitchen roll**

## WHAT TO DO:

Soak the pumpkin seeds. Score the seeds with a fork and set them to one side. Place some small stones in the bottom of the pot for drainage, then fill with compost until around three-quarters full. Place two or three seeds on the soil, spaced evenly, and press them down gently. Cover them with a fine layer of compost and, using a watering can with a fine rose, water them so that the compost is moist but not saturated. Cover the pot with a napkin or a piece of kitchen roll to protect the seeds from the light. Keep the pot in a warm, dark place for a few days and keep the soil moist. As soon as the first tendrils emerge, remove the paper and place the pot on a sunny windowsill.

When the seedlings are strong enough - normally a week after germination - transplant them to a garden bed, ideally in a very sunny position. Pumpkins grow on a long vine, so each plant will need plenty of space. Feed them regularly with a good nitrogen-rich plant food. It won't be long before your first baby pumpkins emerge.

# 61
# CARROT TOPS

Grow a pretty, fernlike plant from the top of a carrot. You won't be able to grow the edible part, but with their white flowers and fronded leaves, carrot tops are hard to beat for speedy growth.

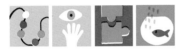

## WHAT YOU'LL NEED:
- **Sharp knife**
- **Carrot (with a little growth of greenery)**
  **Old plate**
- **Small pot**
- **Garden compost**

## WHAT TO DO:
Slice off the top of the carrot about 2.5cm from the crown. Place the carrot top cut-side down on a plate and add some water. Leave it in a warm, sunny position and ensure that there is always plenty of water around the base. Leafy growth will soon start to emerge from the top. When there are at least four or five stems with leaves, transplant it to a plant pot filled with compost. Plant it so that a little of the orange carrot part protrudes above the top of the soil.

# MAKING A GARDEN COMPOSTER

Making your own compost is satisfying and eco-friendly. It will also teach your little one about recycling and the natural process of decomposition.

## WHAT YOU'LL NEED:

- Garden composter with a lid (a plastic rubbish bin will do, with several large holes punched in the sides to allow air to circulate, plus a piece of old carpet if the bin has no lid)
- Twigs, bark, leaves, weeds, fruit and vegetable peelings, coffee grounds, egg shells, tea bags, a good mix of "brown" (e.g., bark and dried leaves) and "green" material (e.g., kitchen scraps and weeds)

## WHAT TO DO:

Chop up the first layer of compost items as finely as you can; the smaller they are, the faster they will decompose. Place them in the bottom of the composter and cover with the lid (or piece of carpet) to retain the heat. Every few days, shake the composter or open it up and stir the contents with a fork. If it becomes too wet, add some sawdust or wood shavings, or a layer of finely shredded newspaper. Many things can be composted, but avoid meat or dairy produce, animal droppings and non-biodegradable materials. Any compost started in spring will be ready for use by autumn. Use it on flowerbeds or in containers to create a healthy home for your plants.

# 63
# PLANTING A BEAN PYRAMID

Plant this green pyramid in late spring and you'll have fresh beans for lunch within six to eight weeks and a lush garden hideout for small children, but hopefully no giant lurking. We love making hideouts with the ivy growing in the garden and this pyramid is even better.

## WHAT YOU'LL NEED:

- Packet of broad bean seeds
- Garden compost
- 5 long bamboo stakes
- Garden twine

## WHAT TO DO:

Prepare the seeds by soaking them in water overnight. Clear a patch of ground about 1 metre square, turn over the soil and dig in a generous quantity of garden compost. Push the bamboo stakes firmly into the ground in a circle, about 10cm inside the edge of the cleared plot. Pull them together at the top to form a pyramid or teepee and tie with some garden twine. Plant the seeds beside the stakes, just inside the pyramid.

Cover them with some more compost and water well. Once the young plants are tall enough, carefully wind them around the stakes and tie them in loosely if necessary. Continue to water daily and watch your bamboo pyramid become a lush new garden den.

# MAKING A HANGING BASKET

This is a great summer activity for kids. They'll enjoy seeing their plants begin to grow and trail over the sides of the basket.

## WHAT YOU'LL NEED:

- **Hanging planter (create your own by tying lengths of sturdy garden twine to the rim of an old basket)**
- **Sphagnum moss**
- **Garden compost**
- **Seedlings or plug plants such as Fuchsia, trailing Geraniums or Petunias, Verbena, Lobelia, Pelargoniums and Alyssum**
- **Watering can with a fine rose**

## WHAT TO DO:

Line the inside of the planter with a layer of moss and soak it with water. Fill it halfway with garden compost. Carefully remove the seedlings from their pots and gently separate the roots with your fingers. Ask your child to help you work out an arrangement for the planter – it's a good idea to have a mix of foliage and flowers – and ensure that each plant has plenty of space in which to grow. Place the plants in position, pack more compost around them and firm it up. When complete, there should be a gap of around 2.5cm between the top of the compost and the top of the planter so that water will soak through and not spill off the top.

Water well and hang the planter in a sunny spot. You'll need to water daily, particularly during hot months. The whole base of the planter can be soaked in a basin of water from time to time. Snip off dead flower heads and feed regularly with plant food to keep the planter looking fresh and healthy.

# GREENHOUSE IN A BOTTLE

Little ones can learn to nurture their own seedlings in this miniature greenhouse.

## WHAT YOU'LL NEED:

- **2 empty 1.5- or 2-litre fizzy drinks bottles, washed**
- **Scissors**
- **Pebbles**
- **Sand**
- **Garden compost**
- **Seedlings (or herb seeds, such as basil)**
- **Watering can with a fine rose**

## WHAT TO DO:

Carefully cut off the top third of each of the drinks bottles, making sure that the edges are smooth and not jagged. Place a layer of pebbles in the bottom of one bottle. Mix together a handful of sand with three handfuls of compost and place it on top of the pebbles. Ask your child to poke several holes in the compost with a finger and carefully plant one seedling in each hole, being careful not to damage the roots (or plant some seeds, see page 97). Gently firm the compost around the seedlings so that they stand upright, adding a little more if need be.

Water the young plants well using the watering can with a fine rose and fit the two bottles together. You may need to make two or three small cuts down the sides of the bottom one so that you can squeeze the sides together slightly and slide the top part down over it. Remember to remove the screw top for the seedlings, as they need oxygen. Placed in a warm, sunny spot, this miniature greenhouse will provide a perfect home for young plants until they are ready to be potted in containers or garden beds.

# Fun with nature

I love the idea of the girls seeing the beauty of the natural world, and they constantly draw my attention to things I may have overlooked, such as the perfect place to create a fairy garden (usually using one of my scarves as a tablecloth for their tea), beautiful leaves and flowers, or a flawless stone that cries out to be painted.

Ava and Hero are always out in the garden collecting "treasures" in order to create lovely gifts to bestow upon me. My dressing table is covered with Ava's little surprises, ranging from pinecones and conkers, to leaf bouquets, shells, pussy willows and even very pretty sticks! Even days out at the beach, or walks in the woods near our house and trips to park provide exciting ingredients for their next project. Don't underestimate what your children can do with some sticks and stones, and what they'll learn in the process!

# STICK BOUQUET

Kids love to pick up twigs and sticks when they're outside. Ask them to look for interesting sticks in a variety of lengths and colours to create an unusual outdoor bouquet.

## WHAT YOU'LL NEED:
- **Twigs and sticks of various shapes, sizes and colours**
- **Garden scissors**
- **Poster paints and brush (optional)**
- **Clay**

## WHAT TO DO:
Brush off any dirt from the sticks and trim off dead leaves or roots. Arrange them on the ground according to size.

If you intend to paint them so that they stand out in the garden, do this now. Once dry, insert the sticks one by one into a lump of clay, arranging them so that they splay out in the form of a bouquet. Once the clay is dry, the bouquet is ready to display.

# FAIRY GARDEN

Stimulate your child's imagination by creating a playground for garden fairies to have fun in when the grown-ups aren't looking.

## WHAT YOU'LL NEED:
You can use just about anything for this project – bits of wool or string to create fairy climbing ropes, or a fairy rope ladder made of string and matchsticks, leaves and flower petals for fairy beds, a lolly stick balanced on a stone for a see-saw, or several glued together to make a tiny table and chairs, pebbles for paths, ivy for tiny fairy bowers, moss for soft play areas and garden walls and fences made with stones and twigs.

## WHAT TO DO:
Why not plant some flower seeds around the borders, to give the fairies somewhere to hide? Discuss what the garden fairies might look like, and what they might need to play happily in their garden. There's no reason why you can't create a fairy garden indoors, too. Every single cotton wool ball in my house has vanished to create Ava's various fairy bowers!

# 68
# PET ROCK

Look out for a rock with interesting shape for your child to keep as a low-maintenance pet. What does it look like? Could you turn it into a dog or a pig? If not, just make it into a comical figure.

## WHAT YOU'LL NEED:
- Suitable rock (washed and dried)
- Acrylic paint and brush
- Googly eyes, glitter, strands of wool, pom poms (see page 87), large buttons, and any anything else that will make your pet unique
- Craft glue

## WHAT TO DO:
Place the rock on some newspaper and paint it. When dry, add some features to give it personality, such as googly eyes, a felt mouth, fabric ears, or a pop pom tail.

Leave your child's new pet in a warm place to dry. How about using scraps of fabric to make it a nice bed? Even pet rocks like a little comfort.

# LEAF RUBBINGS

This is a quick and easy way to make an attractive picture from nature. The principle is the same as for brass rubbing.

## WHAT YOU'LL NEED:
- **2 sheets of white paper**
- **Several different leaves**
- **Wax crayons, paper wrapping removed**

## WHAT TO DO:
Place one sheet of paper on a flat surface. Position the leaves on the paper in an attractive arrangement, with the veins of the leaves facing upwards. Line up the second sheet of paper with the first and carefully place it on top of the leaves. Hold the paper firmly in place and, using the sides rather than the ends of the crayons, rub them across the paper. Images of the leaves beneath will appear as if by magic! Label the leaves with the names of trees and shrubs they come from, if you know them.

# PRESSED LEAF COLLAGE

Teach your child to recognise different trees and create some beautiful artwork at the same time. Why not make a leaf collage between two sheets of sticky back plastic and use it as a place mat?

## WHAT YOU'LL NEED:
- **Leaves of different colours and shapes**
- **Newspaper**
- **Large, thick book**
- **Craft glue or glue stick**
- **Sheet of plain paper or card**

## WHAT TO DO:
Brush off any dirt or debris from the leaves. Place them individually between sheets of newspaper and insert them between the pages of a heavy book. Place the book in a warm, dry place, such as an airing cupboard, until the leaves have dried out. It will take anything from several days to a couple of weeks, depending on their moisture content. When the leaves are ready to use, remove them carefully from the newspaper, as they will now be fragile.

Apply glue to the backs of the leaves and arrange them on the paper or card to create a collage. Ask your child to write the name of the tree or shrub beneath each one. If you're not sure, there's no shame in resorting to a field guide.

# HANDPRINT TREES

A walk outside will provide the inspiration and the material for this unusual tree collage. With your child's handprints forming the leaves, it will also make a classic keepsake.

## WHAT YOU'LL NEED:
- **Pieces of bark and small sticks or twigs**
- **Sheet of card**
- **Craft glue**
- **Non-toxic paint (in green or autumnal colours)**
- **Paper plates**

## WHAT TO DO:
The bark forms the trunk and the twigs the branches of these mini trees. Glue them in position on the card, not forgetting to allow room at the top for the "leaves".

Pour some paint onto a paper plate (use a different plate for each colour). Ask your child to press the palm of their hand firmly into the paint, and then press it onto the paper around the branches, to create pretty handprint leaves.

# ROCK ART

Collect rocks and stones and paint them in pretty colours to brighten up your garden, or decorate some pot plants with colourful pebbles. Ava is obsessed with rock art, and she's made ladybirds, frogs and even jewel-effect creations that are all over the house and garden.

## WHAT YOU'LL NEED:
- **Rocks, stones and pebbles (any shape or size, although flat stones provide a good surface for painting pictures)**
- **Acrylic paint in several colours**
- **Paintbrush**

## WHAT TO DO:
Wash and dry the stones. Place them on a sheet of newspaper and paint the tops and sides. Allow them to dry before turning them over and painting the other side. Acrylic paint produces a good shiny finish and is water-resistant.

Arrange some painted stones along the edge of a garden border or make a rock rainbow. Paint letters on individual stones and spell out your child's name. Or try something more ambitious and paint a picture or a face on a large stone. Paint small pebbles and arrange them around the base of houseplants as a colourful mulch.

# HAND-PAINTED FLOWERPOTS

This is an easy way to add colour to a garden and involve your little one in some outdoor fun.

## WHAT YOU'LL NEED:

- **Old terracotta pots, washed and dried**
- **Acrylic paints**
- **Paintbrush**

## WHAT TO DO:

No matter what the weather, acrylic paint will not run or fade, so it is perfect for outdoor projects. You could simply paint the pots all over in different colours, but if you are planning to grow plants in them, why not paint a picture of what each will contain - a sunflower, a tomato plant, some mint?

If you have several pots that you normally keep in a row, what about painting one long picture across all of them, such as a sausage dog or a caterpillar?

# OUTDOOR PLAY

**L**ike many people, when the weather is not that great and the easiest option is to just snuggle up on the sofa, I sometimes struggle to get out of the house. And, yet, when I do make the effort, it makes me realise that I should do it more often.

I love seeing the girls running around in the park, and now that Ava is bigger, we have started climbing trees! We organise treasure hunts (which might include the odd fairy) and draw up checklists of things to look for while we are out, such as a dog with floppy ears, a red car, a duck pond, etc. Despite the often rather impromptu nature of our plans we usually have great adventures, but I won't divulge where we see our fairies!

Our activities are often very simple, such as learning to ride bikes, playing Poohsticks or blowing bubbles, or we might cover a nearby pavement with coloured chalk – perhaps a touch old fashioned, but fun and creative and it washes away in seconds. At the moment we are building a den with branches and twigs near our new house, and it's a great place to hide from "bears"!

In other words, outdoor play can be as spontaneous and simple as you like. As one activity develops into another and you find new things to explore and do, you'll begin to value the time you spend outdoors, in any weather! In this chapter, you'll find lots of ideas for things to do outside, which is useful for when you are stuck for inspiration or for when a suggestion to play one of your usual games is not met with much enthusiasm. Some are based on the things I used to do when I was a child; others have been inspired through play with my own girls, or watching other children in action.

Frankly, though, it's just nice to be outside, running about, clearing your head, getting fresh air and exercise, and just having a change of scene. We all need to do that from time to time!

*Myleene*
*x*

# SHADOW TRACING

You may remember playing this game when you were little. If you enjoyed it, your children probably will too. It's simple, fun and creative. It's also an opportunity to teach children about how their shadow changes depending on the position of the sun.

## WHAT YOU'LL NEED:

- Coloured chalk or thick marker pens and paints
- Large sheet(s) of plain paper

## WHAT TO DO:

On a sunny day, ask your child to stand still long enough for you to trace around their shadow on the ground. Chalk works well on a paved or tarmacked surface and will ultimately wash off, or you can stand your little one in front of a large sheet of paper and use a marker pen. Your child can then colour in their shadow image with chalk or paint, which will be far less stressful exercise when outside and away from precious furniture and flooring.

Get them to hold their hands above their heads, or adopt funny positions to create comical shadows. Or they can trace around your shadow, though you'll need a bigger piece of pavement or paper!

# 75

# A HAVEN FOR BIRDS

Children are fascinated by birds, probably because they can never get close enough to these elusive creatures to examine them properly. Here are two ideas to attract birds to your garden. Remember that once you start feeding them you'll need to continue, as they'll come to depend upon you as a food source, especially in winter.

## WHAT YOU'LL NEED:
- ½ empty litre juice carton, washed and dried
- Scissors
- Straight twig or stick from the garden, around 20cm long
- Bird seed
- Garden twine

## WHAT TO DO:
Using the scissors, cut two feeding holes around 4cm in diameter in opposite sides of the carton, about half way up. Using the point of the scissors, pierce a small hole beneath each large one and push the twig through the holes so that it protrudes to make a perch on either side.

Pierce some tiny holes in the base of the carton to allow any rainwater to drain away, but not large enough to let the bird seed drop through. Fill the carton with bird seed, right up to the feeding holes. Now squeeze the top edges of the carton together and pierce two holes right through them, about 6cm apart. Thread a length of garden twine through the holes so that you can hang the feeder from a tree. If the top edges of the carton fall open, keep them closed with a couple of pegs or paper clips. When the feeder becomes grubby and worn, just make a new one.

# BIRD FEED BALLS
Another way to feed the birds!

## WHAT YOU'LL NEED:
- **Several plastic cups or empty yoghurt pots, washed**
- **Several lengths of garden twine**
- **100g shredded suet**
- **100g bird seed**
- **Handful of fresh, unsalted, raw peanuts, sunflower seeds and/or stale breadcrumbs**

## WHAT TO DO:
Prepare the cups or pots by piercing a hole in the bottom of each and threading through a length of garden twine. Make a large knot in the end below the bottom of the cup to secure it. Melt the suet in a small saucepan over low heat. Once it has become liquid, stir in the bird seed and other dry ingredients. Continue stirring until everything is well combined, then press some of the suet mixture into the bottom of each of the cups. Make sure that the twine remains in the centre and press the mixture down around it.

Leave the balls in a cool place to set - it usually takes about a day - or speed up the process by putting them in the refrigerator. When set, cut away the cups or pots to release the contents. Tie them to the branches of trees and shrubs, but make sure they are out of reach of cats or rodents, and enjoy watching and identifying your new garden visitors.

# 77

# BAT THE BALLOON

Playing outside with leftover balloons from birthday parties is great fun on a sunny day. Just make sure you have lots to hand, or there may be tears when they land among the roses.

## WHAT YOU'LL NEED:
- **Empty 1-litre water bottles or children's racquets or foam bats, if you have them**
- Balloons

## WHAT TO DO:
Try balloon tennis by batting a balloon back and forth over a "net" made of a couple of garden chairs placed on their sides, end to end, or one long folding sunbed. You may not serve any aces, but you should be able to get a good rally going.

Or, use garden chairs the right way up and bat a balloon through their legs in a game of balloon croquet. Insert two long bamboo canes in the ground for goal posts and see who can hit their balloon between them first. Make it harder by installing a goalie or making the goal narrower. Give each child a balloon and see who can hit theirs the highest or the furthest, or who can keep theirs up in the air the longest. Balloon games provide cheap and cheerful ways to let off steam or hot air!

# TREASURE HUNT

A treasure hunt is fun, flexible and family-friendly. It can be adapted to suit your children's interests and ages.

## WHAT TO DO:

Make a checklist of suitable things to hunt for wherever you are – at the park, on the beach, or just in the garden. Make the list in picture form for young children, drawing an oak leaf, a conker, a yellow flower, a clam shell, a smooth pebble, and so on. Make it a written one for older children, or, if they are just beginning to read, use both words and pictures. Ask for more than one of some items (three sea shells) to encourage them to count. Provide them with a bag or a bucket to store their finds.

To avoid restricting the hunt to small items, create a checklist to tick off rather than collect physically. Again, you can make the list with just images, words or both, but this time arm each child with a pencil so they can cross off the things they see, such as a black cat, a girl in a red jacket, an apple tree, or a fire engine.

# OBSTACLE COURSE

Children love a challenge and they love running around. Combining the two in an obstacle course is an opportunity to get them outside doing what they do best - using up some of that endless supply of energy - and a recipe for plenty of laughter. (To try one inside on rainy days, see page 148.)

## WHAT TO DO:

Use whatever you have to hand to create a challenging course. Here are some ideas: crawl under a picnic table, or through a tunnel made of garden chairs; perform ten star jumps on the spot; jump over rolled-up towels; walk along a board placed on the floor, if one foot goes on the ground you have to start again; jump in and out of a cardboard box; limbo under a skipping rope tied between two trees or chairs; hop on one foot for the count of fifteen; keep a hula hoop moving for the count of five; push a child's car or wheelbarrow from one end of the garden to another; carry a bucket of water between two markers; bat a balloon in the air five times; throw a beanbag into a bucket from a distance; dribble a football around plastic cones; walk backwards for six steps . . .

Encourage your child to help with ideas for the obstacles and write out the course instructions beforehand in words or pictures, depending on your child's age. They can be taped to each "station". Change the course each time to keep it interesting, and don't forget your stopwatch.

# 80

# HOPSCOTCH

Hopscotch is one of those games that many have played but forget about as soon as childhood is left behind. All you need is a small stone for a marker, a hard, flat surface and some chalk.

WHAT TO DO:
Draw a hopscotch pitch on a path, driveway, patio, or whatever flat surface you can find, and number the squares from one to ten. If you can't remember the traditional layout, or if you want to ring the changes, look on the Internet for different layouts, or ask your child to help you create an original design. Choose a small stone as a marker, and you are ready to play.

The first player throws their marker onto the first square. They hop over that square to land in the second square on one foot. Remember that you may only have one foot in each square at a time. When there are two squares side by side, you must land with one foot in each. The first player must then make their way up the pitch, jumping and hopping on one or two feet depending on the layout of the squares. They turn around at the top and return exactly the same way. When back at square two, they must balance on one foot to pick up the marker from square one, then hop over square one back to the start line.

If a player misses a square, loses their balance, steps on a line, or lands with two feet in a single square, or misses throwing their marker into the correct square, they must stop and their turn is over. Their next turn will begin where their last one ended. If they are successful, they throw their marker into square two, hop into square one, then into square three and carry on up the pitch as before. The first person to complete the whole course, from one to ten, is the winner.

# EGG CARTON BOAT

Rescue an egg carton from the recycling pile and head for the high seas.

## WHAT YOU'LL NEED:
- Egg carton lid
- Aluminium foil
- Sheet of paper
- Scissors
- Wooden skewer, straw or straight twig
- Sticky/masking tape

## WHAT TO DO:
Cover the entire egg carton lid from front and back with aluminium foil, smoothing it down to ensure it is watertight, as this will form the boat's hull. Cut a triangle from the paper for the sail, making each side about 10cm long. Poke two small holes in the sail, one at the top in the apex of the triangle, and one at the bottom. Push the skewer, straw or twig through the bottom hole and then out though the top hole to make the mast. Tape the bottom of the mast to the inside of the boat, making sure it is secure and upright. If using a straw, try making several small cuts in one end, splay them out over the "hull" and tape into position.

Now all you need is a pond, stream, paddling pool or large puddle and a puff of wind to sail off into the horizon.

# SNOW GRAFFITI

Children don't normally need much encouragement to go out and play in the snow, but this activity makes an entertaining change from building snowmen and throwing snowballs.

## WHAT YOU'LL NEED:
- **Red, yellow and blue food colouring**
- **3 empty spray bottles**

## WHAT TO DO:
Make up at least three different colours, with a bottle each of say red, yellow and blue snow paint. Add around ten drops of each food colouring to each bottle – the colour needs to be strong enough to show up clearly on the snow. Fill the bottles with water and place them in the freezer until the water is ice cold but not frozen, it must be very cold or the paint will melt the snow. Now, wrap your child up warmly, choose a pristine piece of snow for a "canvas", arm them with their "snow graffiti" kit, and away they go.

Experiment with the colours. What happens when yellow is sprayed over blue? Or red over yellow? Encourage them to make big, bold pictures and remember to take a photo since these artistic creations will melt eventually.

# ICE PAINTING

This is a gorgeously messy activity that takes a little advance preparation, but produces hours of fun. It's perfect for a hot day when young artists need to cool down a little, and a great way to teach children about primary and secondary colours at the same time.

## WHAT YOU'LL NEED:

- Ice cube tray
- Red, yellow and blue food colouring, or poster paints
- Lolly sticks or wooden ice cream spoons (optional)
- Sheets of craft paper

## WHAT TO DO:

Add six or seven drops of food colouring to each compartment of the ice cube tray. Each cube should be a different colour, so add red colouring to the first compartment, blue to the second, yellow, the third. Then make up some secondary colours, such as blue and yellow to make green, red and blue for purple, red and yellow for orange, red and green for brown, etc. If you are using poster paints, a good dollop in the bottom of each compartment should be sufficient.

Next, fill the tray to the top with water, stirring each compartment well to mix in the colour, and place the tray in the freezer. After about an hour, take it out and insert a lolly stick or wooden ice cream spoon into the semi-frozen water in each compartment. Return the tray to the freezer until the cubes are completely frozen (usually two or three hours). If your little one doesn't mind cold hands, you can miss out this step.

Once the ice is frozen solid, remove the tray and twist it to loosen the paint cubes. Now all young artists need is a sheet of paper and they can paint away outside to their hearts' content. They might need to work more quickly on a very hot day, but speed only adds to the creative impetus!

# 84

# HOME-MADE BUBBLES

There is something quite hypnotic about blowing bubbles –
it's a perfectly good way of whiling away a summer's day, even
for adults! We go through bottles and bottles of home-made
bubble mixture in our house.

## WHAT YOU'LL NEED:
- **150ml washing-up liquid**
- **1 litre of water**
- **2 tbsp glycerine (available in the baking section of the supermarket, or at the chemist)**
- **Pipe cleaner or wire coat hanger, anything to make a wand**

## WHAT TO DO:
Combine the ingredients in a large bowl or pitcher, stirring gently. You don't want too many bubbles at this stage. Leave the mixture to stand for ten minutes or so, to combine and settle, while you make the wand. Pipe cleaners can be bent into effective small wands, and a wire coat hanger bent into a circle or a heart will make fantastic huge bubbles, providing you have a large enough container for the bubble mixture. In fact, virtually anything with a hole (or holes) that can be blown or waved around will work well. A kitchen straining spoon will create a stream of tiny bubbles when waved through the air, or you could even just use your thumb and forefinger, tips touching in a circle.

Why not play games with bubbles? Whose bubble lasts the longest? How long can you hold a bubble on the palm of your hand before it bursts? How many can you catch and pop, and how many can you blow in one breath?

85

# SKILLS BOOT CAMP

Help your child to master some skills. The ones suggested below may sound rather simple, but it's easy to forget that they represent quite a challenge to very young children and so when mastered create a great sense of pride and achievement.

Can they swing without being pushed? Can they push a wheelbarrow in a straight line or dig a hole 30cm deep? Help them to make a sandcastle, or create a fairy garden (see page 108). Learn how to ride a tricycle or a two-wheeled bike. Or what about gym skills such as touching your toes, a forward roll, and climbing to the top of a climbing frame or a rope?

Or, what about bouncing a ball on the spot for as long as possible, hitting a tennis ball over a net, or balancing a ball on a racquet while running? Make the skills more challenging for older children. For example, do they like football? Useful soccer skills include kicking a ball into a goal, dribbling past an opponent and "keepy-uppy" (seeing how long you can you keep a ball in the air with your feet and knees).

# 86

# WHACKY RACES

The idea is for several children to compete against one another in a mini Olympics, or for a child playing alone to try for a personal best.

WHAT TO DO:

If your children can't find anything to do in the garden, why not challenge them with a series of races? Try these, for example: hop a certain number of times on one foot; hop forwards four steps and then backwards four steps; skip ten times on the spot with a skipping rope (or, for younger members of the family, skip without a rope around the garden several times); jump over several empty cardboard boxes, hurdle-style; do a hop-skip-and-jump (triple jump) in a sandbox or on the lawn and mark the jumping off point with a couple of upturned flower pots.

Challenge children to "run" the length of the lawn or garden on their knees, or on their heels or tiptoe, or shuffle along on their bottom (check the course for sharp stones first), or walk it backwards or hopping on one leg; hold a "wheelbarrow" race (one child holds the legs of another who walks along on their hands); run with a beanbag on your head without it falling off; or what about an old-fashioned egg-and-spoon race, using hardboiled eggs of course.

# HOSEPIPE SLIDE

You need a stretch of grass for this. It works best on a gentle incline, so if you have a slope in your garden you are off to a good start. If not, children will still have fun swooshing along a flat stretch of grass, being active but keeping cool in the summer sunshine.

## WHAT YOU'LL NEED:
- **Groundsheet or some thick plastic bin liners**
- **Bubble bath**
- **Hose pipe and water**

## WHAT TO DO:
Make sure that there are no sharp stones or protrusions in the grass that could injure your child or rip the plastic sheeting. Lay the sheeting on the ground or place several bin liners together, end to end, and tape them together. Make sure the taped joins are smooth so that little feet cannot get caught up in them. Line the sides with stones to keep the sheets in place (particularly if it's windy) or use tent pegs to secure them in place. Make sure you have a good wide space in the middle for sliding. If the bin liners are thick enough, you could cut them open down one side to make them double width.

Pour some bubble bath over the surface of the sheeting and position the nozzle of a hosepipe at the top. Turn it on to create a rush of bubbly water down a slippery slide.

# 88

# FLIP A COIN ADVENTURE

Most children react to the idea of going for a healthy walk with a distinct lack of enthusiasm, at least without the prospect of an interesting destination (to them) at the end of it. If your little ones tend to drag their feet when you want to take them out for a nice long walk, try turning it into a mystery tour.

WHAT TO DO:

Take a coin or dice with you and when you reach a junction, flip the coin for right (heads) or left (tails), flip heads twice in succession for straight on. Or roll the dice to see which turning to take or decide how many more minutes you should walk in a particular direction. See where chance takes you and try not to get lost. You might need to cheat if little legs start to get tired.

**89**

# TEDDY BEARS' PICNIC

There is nothing nicer than eating al fresco, particularly in the company of teddy bears. A teddy bear (or soft toy) picnic is always popular with children. Get them busy in the kitchen beforehand, preparing easy picnic treats. Ask them to spread jam and butter on bread for sandwiches, wash some grapes and cherry tomatoes, and wrap up chunks of cheese. Don't forget to make some fairy cakes topped with gummy bears or Rice Krispie® teddies for dessert (see page 222). Add a bottle of home-made pink lemonade (see page 232), pack it all up and head to your local park with some rugs or towels to sit on, and, of course, the teddies. Don't forget the plastic plates and cutlery for both you and your teddy guests. Your young host or hostess may like to make some invitations for everyone, too. The more there is to do to prepare for the picnic, the more special it will be.

# 90

# SPRINKLER DODGE 'EMS

Much fun is to be had with the humble garden sprinkler in the warmer months and if you play your cards right, your children won't need a bath before bedtime, either!

## WHAT TO DO:

**OBSTACLE COURSE:** Include a sprinkler in an obstacle course (see page 126). The challenge is to jump over it or run through the spray. Play catch with water balloons thrown through the sprinkler and see how difficult it is to catch them when they are wet. See how long they can stand still under the spray before they get too cold and give in! Set your timer!

**IMPROMPTU BODY ART:** Use a sponge painting set and finger or face paints to decorate one another, and then run through the sprinkler to wash them off.

**WASHING UP:** Get children to wash down their tricycles, bikes and ride-on vehicles with a sponge and soapy water (see opposite), and then run them through the sprinkler for a final rinse.

**BATH TIME:** Wash your kids all over with some child-friendly shower gel or baby bath, and encourage them to run back and forth until they are squeaky clean and the soap has all washed away. And that way they won't need a bath!

**GARDEN SLIDE:** Place a sprinkler at the bottom of a slide and let the children whizz through it as they slide down. Or position it near a swing, so that they can swing into the water as they go back and forth. Set it up to sprinkle over a hosepipe slide (see page 136) to make the course more slippery.

**PLAY DODGE-THE-SPRINKLER:** Man the tap and turn the water off and on (or up and down) in a random pattern. See how close your children can get without being caught.

# WHAT'S THAT BUG?

Investigating creepy-crawlies in the garden or park introduces children to nature at an early age and may help to stave off any learned phobic behaviour, such as a fear of spiders.

WHAT TO DO:
There's a number of simple things you can do both on a "field trip" and at home. Draw or take photographs (a "bugshot") of each insect and stick them in a scrapbook. Research on the Internet to identify them and label your bug images. Make a note of any interesting facts, such as the number of legs or eyes, preferred habitat, does it have wings? Make a checklist of insects you'd like to find and hunt for them – a ladybird, a butterfly, a snail, a black beetle, a spider . . . What would your child call the bugs they find? A crawly-saurus? A flutterby? Willy woodlouse? See if you can make up some silly names for them to write beneath their "scientific" names.

Keep some bugs for a short period of time for close observation, but make sure they have sufficient air, such as in a jar with holes poked in the lid, or topped with pierced cling film. And make sure they have something to eat and drink. Check their habits and diet on the Internet, but if they turn out to be fussy eaters demanding only Michelin-starred bug cuisine (or other bugs!), it would be best to repatriate them immediately. Look out for a caterpillar; if you are lucky, you might see it turn into a moth or butterfly. When your observations are complete, remember to release the bugs back into the garden, in a similar place to where you found them if possible.

92

# CAR WASH

Washing the family car, or your child's own bike or ride-on car, is actually very good exercise. All you need is a bucket of nice warm, soapy water, some rubber gloves and some nice big sponges.

Make sure the detergent is child-friendly as there is bound to be plenty of splashing going on. Allocate the bottom half of the car to your child to make things easier, and be prepared to refill buckets frequently. The chances are the car won't be washed perfectly, but for entertainment value, this activity can't be beaten.

# INDOOR
# PLAY

**I**ndoor play is what I love best. I'm a total homebody and I like nothing better than to have my babies playing in the house and running riot with their friends!

You don't have to buy expensive toys or plug your kids into a computer or TV to keep them happy at home. All you need is their imagination, a pile of blankets and all the cushions from the sofa – we love to build dens.

When I was a child, nothing gave me more pleasure than taking all the cushions from the dining room chairs and arranging them around the table to make a secret cave. And if my mum let me eat my dinner in there, even better! Now I help my girls to build dens in the living room and in their bedrooms. I let them raid my wardrobe, dress up as princesses, fairies or monsters and then create a castle from anything we can find and hide there until tea time.

Hide-and-seek is also pretty popular in our house (if in doubt, both girls can nearly always be found giggling behind the curtains), as is "going shopping". Ava makes the list and pushes her toy buggy as a trolley. Hero puts the shopping in it and I play the checkout girl. Uncomplicated, good old-fashioned play is so underrated. You have the opportunity to laugh and spend time with your children, and discover how they think and actually view the world around them. For example, when playing "mummies and babies" there's nothing scarier than hearing your little one repeat back to you the things you say to them. *Do I really sound like that*?

Myleene
x

# Little helpers around the house

Indoor play also gives children a chance to see how the household runs and how the family functions as a unit within it. Here are some suggestions to get your little one helping around the house, and enjoy it!

● Running a household involves good teamwork. If your children feel that they are an important part of that team, with a star chart to reward effort and a good work, you are well on your way to encouraging self-sufficient children.

● Making games of chores makes them more fun and children learn a lot by taking on even simple tasks, like dividing laundry into colours for the washing machine and watering the houseplants.

● When it's time to clean the house, arm your children with dusters, an apron, a spray bottle with water and a squeeze of lemon juice, a cloth, a dustpan or a small damp mop, and a list (in pictures or words) of things to do. Even if it's not perfect (or even remotely clean), it's the concept of helping that is important.

● Give your child a plant to care for, and explain how to check the soil to see if it needs a bit more water. If you have pets, show your child how to measure out the dry food and place it in your pets' bowls.

● Encourage your child to clear up after their games are finished. Both Hero and Ava have little jobs they like to do, and we often make a game of putting away the toys - racing to see who can clear away their pile first or timing ourselves to beat our previous personal bests.

● Encourage children to pull up their duvets or bedspreads in the morning, and pop their PJs under their pillow or in a pyjama bag. If keeping things clean and tidy becomes part of the routine, children are more likely to do it automatically.

# DENS AND TENTS

Our favourite activity, for sure. We have created dens everywhere in the house, with some spectacular successes and failures. Try not to worry about the mess. If you can keep your children active, engaged and playing happily for hours, an empty airing cupboard may not be such a bad outcome.

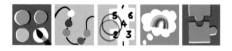

WHAT TO DO:
The indoor world is your oyster. Gather cushions from chairs and sofas to furnish tents made from blankets, tablecloths and towels draped over ropes strung between chair backs. Clothes pegs are handy for sealing entrances and doorstops and books for weighing down the edges. Or use a large cardboard box or a blanket draped over a table. Pull the end of a curtain out from the wall and drape it over the back of a chair. Make use of sleeping bags, play tunnels, clothes horses, airing rails . . . See what your children can come up with to create the perfect hideaway. Serve food on small plates, play some soft music and let them relax in their own cosy space.

# OBSTACLE COURSES

Helping lively kids burn off excess energy on days when going outside is just out of the question can be a real challenge. An indoor obstacle course could be the answer. Any safe, open space (or even the whole house) can host a challenging course.

WHAT TO DO:
Here are some ideas: Create obstacles with furniture, pillows, blankets, piles of books, the kitchen broom . . . Crawl under and over chairs, slide down the stairs on your bottom. Create activity stations where each contestant must jump up and down ten times, perform sit-ups, run on the spot to the count of twenty, do a forward roll.

Or why not mark out a hopscotch pitch in masking tape and hop and jump along it, keep a hula hoop up or bat a balloon in the air for a minute, throw a beanbag into the laundry basket from a distance, walk along a masking tape tightrope, race toy cars from one end of the kitchen table to the other, jump on mum's bed, do a silly dance in the hall, crawl on tummies under a duvet on the floor. Whatever you like!

# 95

# MUSICAL CUSHIONS

It's true that there isn't much to this game. It tends be played at parties and forgotten about for home play, but children love it.

WHAT TO DO:

Arrange the cushions on the floor; there should be one less than the number of children playing. Start the music and encourage the children to dance around the cushions. Stop the music after a short time and they must all rush to sit down on the nearest cushion. The child who ends up without a cushion is out of the game. Start the music again and continue in the same way until there is only one child left – the proud winner.

If you're trying to keep just one child occupied, play musical statues instead. Tell your child to do a silly dance to the music and when it stops they must remain completely still for a count of ten, in whatever weird position they find themselves. You don't need to have a winner for this game and you will probably both be collapsing in giggles sooner or later.

To keep the kids occupied indoors, other party games ideas could include: What Time Is It Mr Wolf? (great for learning to tell the time and for numeracy in general); Simon Says (good for attentive listening); and, when you need a few moments of peace, Sleeping Lions (also good for calming children after too much excitement).

# 96

# SHADOW CREATURES

Impress your children with some shadow animals. Older children can join in and create their own beasts. Why not use animals to tell a story?

## WHAT TO DO:

All you need is a torch or a desk lamp to throw a beam onto a wall in a darkened room, and, of course, your hands. Once you have shown them how, ask your little one to try while you hold the torch. Here are two of the easiest creatures for young children to begin with. Or perhaps you can make up some of your own?

SHADOW DOG

SHADOW BIRD

# BIN BASKETBALL

You don't need to be a tall, gangly basketball player to play this version of the game. All you need is a rubbish bin, which can double up as a basket.

WHAT TO DO:
Place the bin against a wall and position two or three markers (a ruler or a couple of pencils will do) on the floor at varying distances away from the bin. Each player must stand behind a marker and try to throw the ball or beanbag into the basket. Award one point for successful shots from the first and closest marker ("slam dunk"), two points for successful shots from the next shooting position (a bit further away from the basket) and three points from the furthest position. Encourage children to make use of the wall as a backboard (which helps them to work out angles) or make it more difficult by moving the bin away from the wall, so shots have to be exactly on target.

When it's time to tidy up and you find your children are reluctant to take part, try making a game out of it. Ask them to throw their toys (robust ones only) and any rubbish into their respective bins, and award points for accuracy and helpfulness.

# GONE FISHING

Test your child's agility and co-ordination with this fishing game.
See how many fish you can catch with your magnetic fishing rod.

## WHAT YOU'LL NEED:

- Sheet of paper
- Felt-tip pen
- Several sheets of fairly thick coloured card
- Scissors
- Crayons, colouring pens or glitter glue
- Paperclips
- Sticky tape
- Sturdy string
- Short bamboo canes or dowel rods, one per fishing rod
- Magnets, one for each rod (or a recycled fridge magnet)
- Blue, green or white blanket or towel, a bin liner or baby bath, for a pond

## WHAT TO DO:

Begin by drawing the shape of a fish on a sheet of paper to form a template. You will need to cut out a few of these so keep it simple. Make sure it is at least 12cm long or it will be difficult to catch. Using the template, cut out a minimum of 10 fish from the card and decorate them with crayons and glitter.

Tape a paperclip to the tip of each fish's nose, so that about half of the paperclip protrudes beyond the fish. Make the fishing rods. You may not need one for every player, as one or two could be shared between several fishermen, depending upon what game you are playing, Cut a length of sturdy string and tie one end to the fishing rod (the bamboo or dowel rod) and the other to the magnet.

Now it's time to dig an indoor pond, speedily improvised in the form of a blue towel or a bin liner placed on the floor in a pond shape, or even a baby bath or child's empty paddling pool. Number the fish so that children can practise basic maths as well as fishing skills and throw them (the fish!) into the pond. See how many your little one can catch within a time limit.

Or, if you made more than one rod, see who the first to catch five is. The catch can then be sorted and counted, or the numbers on the fish can be added up.

Write the letters of your child's name on the fish so they can catch themselves! Vary the rules to suit the ages of your children – the winner is the first to catch all the red fish, for example, or fish with numbers that add up to ten. Have fun and get in a little sneaky numbers practice when you can.

# 99 BEANBAG FUN

The humble beanbag can be used in all sorts of activities and games to entertain and encourage motor development. Even simply tossing a beanbag back and forth between you is good for hand-eye co-ordination and helps to burn off steam on a rainy day. Create a beanbag course out of empty boxes, rubbish bins, baskets and empty food containers. Number each one and play the course like a game of mini-golf. Throw a beanbag into the first container. Stand next to that "hole", throw the beanbag into number two, and so on. Make the holes more challenging by lengthening the distance between them. Can anyone get a hole in one?

Organise a series of beanbag challenges. Try these: Throw the beanbag up in the air and catch it – first with your hands in front of you and then catch it behind you; clap your hands together once before you catch it, then twice, or clap them behind your back; throw the beanbag in the air and crouch down to the ground and then get up again before you catch it. How many times can you catch it without dropping it? See how far you can walk with a beanbag balanced on your head or with one on each shoulder. Can you catch the beanbag on your foot? Can you jump, climb stairs, dance or perform a star jump with a beanbag (or two) on your head?

# PUPPET PLAY

Puppets are fun to both make and to play with. Children can write their own plays with a little help from you or act out a favourite story. Be prepared for long, rambling performances without an obvious beginning or end! And of course, puppets need a venue, so the first task is to make a theatre. A large cardboard box is ideal.

WHAT YOU'LL NEED:
- **Large cardboard box**
- **Craft knife and scissors**
- **Sticky tape or brown parcel tape**
- **Fabric, to make curtains**
- **Needle and thread or iron-on hemming tape**
- **Dowel rod, long enough to make curtain rail**
- **Poster paints and brush, to decorate (optional)**

WHAT TO DO:
Cut off all the flaps from one side of the box but leave any other flaps in place and firmly tape them shut. The box should be completely open on one side only, which will form the back of the theatre. Cut out a rectangular or square window in the side opposite the back of the theatre (the open end). It should begin 3-4cm down from the top edge and be large enough for the puppets to "act" in. This will be the front of the theatre.

Now make some curtains. Cut a length of fabric the same size as the window at the front, but making it slightly longer than necessary to accommodate the hem you are about to make. Fold down the top of the fabric to create a hem wide enough to thread the dowel rod through.

Sew the hem in place or use hemming tape and cut the fabric in half to form two curtains. Cut two holes on either side of the box, 2-3cm from the front of the theatre and just above the top of the window. Slide the dowel rod through one of the holes, then thread the curtains onto the dowel and slide the end of the dowel through the hole in the other side of the box. The curtains should now be in position.

Paint the outside of the box to make the theatre bright and colourful. Children can access it through the open end at the back and manipulate their puppets in the window. Add the finishing touch by painting your theatre's name on the front (The Puppet Palace) and make a small poster to advertise what's "showing tonight" or who is starring "direct from the West End".

# MAKING PUPPETS

Puppets can be made out of virtually anything, as long as you have a good supply of craft materials. Here are a few ideas:

## WHAT TO DO:

**FINGER PUPPETS:** Cut the fingers off a pair of cotton gloves (or rubber gloves for an impromptu puppet show in the bath), and draw on faces using a permanent marker pen. Stick on some googly eyes and wool for hair and allow to dry.

**HAND PUPPETS:** While you don't want to encourage your child to draw on their hands, this is an easy way to create an almost instant puppet with virtually no materials. Ask your little one to ball their hand into a fist, and draw on some eyes, eyebrows, a nose, a mouth and some hair using washable felt-tip pens. Show your little one how to move their thumb and fingers to make it look like their puppet is talking.

**SOCK PUPPETS:** Choose an old, clean sock and place it over your child's hand – the toe of the sock should sit over their four fingers, held upright, and the heel over their thumb – this will form the bottom lip or jaw. Get them to close their hand so that their fingers meet their thumb. Now the puppet's mouth is closed, so you can mark where the eyes, nose and ears will be with a felt-tip pen. Take the sock off your child's hand and stick or sew on its features: pieces of felt for ears and a nose, beads or buttons for eyes (or googly eyes). Small pieces of white felt make good teeth and red felt becomes a nice long tongue, while wool is perfect for eyelashes and hair, and pipe cleaners can be bent into ears.

**LOLLY STICK PUPPETS:** Use wooden spoons or lolly sticks to create a whole collection of small puppet characters. Draw faces and stick on bits of fabric, felt, wool and anything else you have to hand to create clothing and hair. Aluminium foil makes lovely tiaras and crowns; a piece of paper napkin is the perfect cape; cut out legs, arms, wings, horns, petals, and so on, from craft foam to give your puppet character.

# Dressing up and role play

Ava and Hero adore dressing up and absolutely love the opportunity to be someone else for a few hours (or in extreme cases, whole days). I know it's good for them, too. Dressing up is fun and gives children the chance to use their imagination and to imitate both what they read about in books and see in the world around them.

The same goes for role play. Playing shop, restaurant, post office or doctor and nurse may not seem very interesting to adults, but in acting out what they have seen, children are expressing their experiences verbally and thinking things through in a way that aids their development. They have fun while also learning to solve problems and consolidate their knowledge of the world.

When children play together, they learn co-operation and social skills, and develop confidence. They use their imagination to dream up scenarios and improvise and act them out. Giving your children lots of materials to enrich their playtime increases their enjoyment. Create masks and costumes and invent scenarios together; make or buy puppets and put on a show. Make the most of role play by re-enacting experiences that have troubled them and talking about their concerns and fears. You may get some insight into the things that matter most to them.

# PLAY SHOP

Stock a play shop with tins, packets, fruit and vegetables from your own larder or buy children's plastic versions. Provide some carrier bags for those customers who have not brought their own. A child's wagon or pushchair makes a perfect supermarket trolley, boxes with drawers make good cash registers, and you can make your own loyalty, debit and credit cards to "swipe" under a calculator or use play coins and paper money. Don't forget to sticker the stock with prices and make sure you write out a shopping list first. What's your "buy one get one free" deal this week?

# PLAY KITCHEN

If you are not feeling up to a full cooking session, set up a play kitchen in a corner. Big boxes make great ovens and refrigerators (tape flaps shut and cut open one side for a door), and old oven gloves, aprons and tea towels can be put to good use, along with sponges, plastic utensils, bowls, pots, pans, plates and child-friendly cutlery. You probably won't want real food served from a play kitchen, so this is one occasion where the plastic stuff is probably best. A washing-up bowl makes a perfect sink, and you can rifle the recycling bin for old jars and food packets to stock the store cupboard.

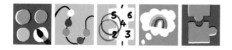

# 104

# PLAY POST OFFICE

Prepare some items to sell, such as stamps drawn on sticky-backed labels, and rescue junk mail envelopes from the recycling. Gather some twine, brown paper and sticky tape for wrapping parcels, and use the kitchen scales to weigh them. Write a few postcards and letters to take to the post office counter. Does your post office sell vehicle tax discs (cut a few circles out of paper), or have a bureau de change (paper cut into euro or dollar notes)? And don't forget your home-made postbox (see page 66). A postman's sack (hessian shopping bag) will complete the look when your child collects the contents of the postbox.

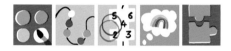

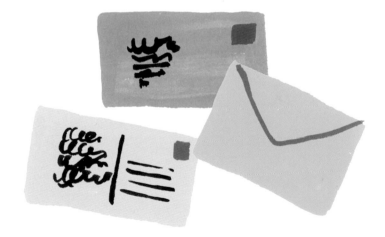

# 105

# PRINCESS OR PRINCE FOR THE DAY

Becoming a princess or a prince is a favourite fantasy of many little ones and this activity offers them a chance to act it out! Hunt through the dressing-up box together, what would a prince or princess wear? Make up a location for the castle and draw a map of her or his kingdom. What would a princess or prince have for breakfast? Can you rustle up some royal food together? Read some appropriate fairy tales together (see page 25) and re-enact them. Does your princess feel the pea under the mattress? Can she change that frog back into a prince? Can your prince wake Sleeping Beauty with a kiss or save Rapunzel from her tower? Anything and everything you can do to excite your child's imagination will add to the fun and make it a day to remember.

# EASY CAPES

Old sheets or towels can be cut up and used to form impromptu capes, or make your own as described below and decorate it. How about adding a royal touch with some fake fur trim around the edge? I'm no seamstress, but I've made several of these capes and you can make one in under an hour.

## WHAT YOU'LL NEED:

- Approx. 1 metre of fabric
- Measuring tape
- Scissors
- Iron-on hemming tape
- 1 metre of ribbon, approx. 3cm in width
- Fabric paints, sequins, glitter, feathers and buttons, to decorate
- Craft glue

## WHAT TO DO:

Measure your princess or wizard from shoulder to knee, and cut the fabric to the appropriate length, adding extra for a hem at the neck. Measure a 7.5cm hem at the top of the cape. Fold it down and iron it flat. Now unfold it and place the ribbon on the fabric just below the fold. Make sure it lies flat. Cut a piece of hemming tape the same length as the hem and place it just below the ribbon so that it sits at the point where the bottom edge of the hem meets the fabric.

Fold down the top of the hem over the ribbon and tape and pass a hot iron over the tape to seal the hem (follow the manufacturer's instructions; you may need to cover it with a damp cloth). Use further lengths of hemming tape to create a narrow hem around the remaining three sides of the cape if you wish. Alternatively, cut around the edges with pinking shears to stop them from fraying, or just leave them as they are.

# HOME-MADE FACE PAINT

Turn your little one into a tiger, a pirate, a fairy. Or start with more basic effects, as you don't need to be an expert to draw something simple, such as a moustache or a pretty butterfly on a little cheek. Prepare several lots of paint in different colours and use make-up sponges and soft, clean paintbrushes (old make-up brushes work well, but give them a good wash first). Work in layers, allowing each to dry before moving on to the next.

## WHAT YOU'LL NEED:

- **2 tsp cornflour**
- **1 tsp water**
- **1 tsp cold cream (e.g. Pond's)**

### FOR OVERALL WHITE BASE:

- **4 tsp vegetable fat**
- **10 tsp cornflour**
- **1 tsp plain flour**
- **2 drops of food colouring (optional)**

## WHAT TO DO:

Blend together 2 tsp conflour with the water and cold cream, and decant into a small jar with an airtight lid. Shake well.

For an overall white base, add in the vegetable fat, along with 10 tsps of cornflour and the plain flour. If you want to add hint of colour, put in 2 drops of food colouring, but go easy! A little goes a long way. Apply with a clean, damp sponge, taking care around the eyes, nose and mouth.

This recipe will keep for about a month, in a small sealed jar in the fridge. Prepare several lots of paint in different colours and always use clean brushes when applying it.

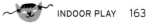

# 108

# DRESSING-UP BOXES

A well-stocked dressing-up box can provide hours of fun but you don't need to fill it with expensive shop-bought costumes. All sorts of things that you might ordinarily throw away or donate to the charity shop can be put to good dressing-up use, starting with the most obvious, such as clothes, shoes, hats and perhaps jewellery. But why stop there when old towels and scarves can be turned into capes and turbans, or plastic bowls and colanders to make hats or helmets?

Don't overlook accessories such as empty perfume bottles, old handbags or briefcases, rucksacks, aprons, belts, sunglasses or prescription glasses with the lenses removed, feather boas, old mobile phones, keys, walking sticks, gloves. Headbands can be adapted with feathers, glitter, aluminium foil, etc., to form a variety of different headgear. The inserts of wrapping-paper tubes make perfect magic wands and light sabres. Chopsticks are ideal for conducting an orchestra or as magic wands, a magnifying glass and notepad are must-haves for a detective on the hunt for clues, and an old pair of dungarees will be a hit with a budding mechanic or train driver. What about adding empty water bottles and old toothbrushes for the new dental surgery? The more, the better!

# 109

# FAIRY WINGS

These versatile wings don't need to be confined to fairies.
They they can be adapted for less refined creatures too, such
as a scary monster or Count Dracula. They are simple to make,
so create several sets for the dressing-up box if you have time.

## WHAT YOU'LL NEED:

- **Thick aluminium wire from a craft shop (usually sold on a spool and cut to your requirement)**
- **Duct tape**
- **Pair of women's tights (sheer or white for fairies; black for a more sinister character)**
- **Elastic**
- **Sequins, ribbon, glitter, buttons, to decorate**
- **Craft glue**

## WHAT TO DO:

Shape the wire into a large circle, about the height of your child from shoulder to hip. Tape the ends together firmly with duct tape, making sure there are no sharp bits to scratch little arms. Twist the circle in the centre so that it becomes a figure "8" and fasten it securely with duct tape. You now have two loops of wire that will form the wings. Bend each into a nice wing shape, making it pointy like a butterfly, round or scalloped, whatever takes your fancy.

Cut off the legs from a pair of tights and stretch one leg over each wing. Pull the legs taught, knot them at the centre of the wings and cut off the excess. Cut two pieces of elastic large enough to fit over your child's shoulders, and tie or sew them to the centre of the wings. Decorate the wings to suit a particular costume or character, or just to make them unique.

# MASKS

Masks add the finishing touch to a costume, or can be a quick and easy way to create a particular character or look without a lot of dressing up. Paint them to resemble animals, people, scary things, or whatever you like.

## WHAT YOU'LL NEED:
- **Newspaper, cut into strips, and some to cover your work surface**
- **Round balloon (have a few spare, just in case one pops)**
- **Felt-tip pen**
- **Large bowl**
- **Plain flour**
- **Water**
- **Brush for glue**
- **Poster paints and brush**
- **Decorations as required**
- **Elastic**

## WHAT TO DO:
Cover your work surface with several sheets of old newspaper, as this gets very messy. Blow up the balloon to about the size of your child's head and tie the end closed. Using a felt-tip pen, mark out the shape of the mask on the balloon. A mask to cover the whole face will normally cover around half the balloon, lengthways, and as well as spaces for two eyes and a mouth. Mix up some paste in the bowl, using 2 parts water to 1 part flour (2 mugs of water to 1 mug of flour is normally enough to create one mask).

Place the balloon on a small dish to prevent it rolling around while you are working. Dip a newspaper strip into the paste for several seconds so that it is saturated, allow the excess to drip off and place it over the balloon, smoothing out any creases with a brush. Dip another strip in the paste and repeat the process and carry on until the whole of the mask is covered.

Apply a second layer of newspaper over the first, placing the strips so they are running in a different direction (i.e. if you placed them mostly going across the balloon in the first layer, now place them going vertically). When you have applied two layers of newspaper, leave the mask to dry for at least two or three hours, in a warm place if possible to speed up the process. While the mask is drying, cover the remaining paste with a damp towel or some cling film to avoid it drying out.

Once the mask has dried a little, apply another two layers of newspaper, then allow those to dry and carry on until you have applied around 6 or 7 layers. Features like eyebrows, lips, noses, ears and witches' warts can be created by rolling or scrunching up pieces of newspaper, dunking them in the paste and sticking them to the mask, but don't saturate these with paste to the point where they start to disintegrate. Apply a couple of flat strips of paper over the features to create a smooth, "skin" finish if you like. Leave the completed mask to dry out in a warm place – it may take a couple of days.

When it's dry, paint and/or decorate the mask, then pop the balloon by pressing the tip of a pair of scissors into the mouth area and remove the pieces. Carefully pierce a hole on either side of the mask and attach a length of elastic long enough to go round your child's head. Alternatively, staple the elastic in place. Now all you need is an invitation to a masked ball!

# WANDS

Wands are easy to make. The trick is to decorate them as extravagantly as you can.

## WHAT YOU'LL NEED:

- **Sheet of paper**
- **Scissors**
- **Sheet of thin craft foam**
- **Glue**
- **Piece of bamboo or a dowel rod, around 30cm in length**
- **Poster paint (metallic paints are ideal, or go for something spookily black or deliciously pink)**
- **Paintbrush**
- **Multicoloured ribbons (optional)**
- **Glitter glue, sequins, anything sparkly to decorate**

## WHAT TO DO:

Draw a nice big star on the paper and cut it out to form a template. Use the template to cut out two stars from the craft foam. Cover one side of each star with glue and press them together over 2-3cm of one end of the bamboo or dowel rod. When the glue is dry, paint the wand – you'll need to paint one side first and allow it to dry before turning it over and painting the other. Cut several lengths of ribbon and glue them to the bottom of the star. Allow to dry.

For a really fancy wand, cut out some small stars from the leftover bits of craft foam and glue them to the ends of the ribbons. Decorate the star with glitter glue, sequins and anything else sparkly for extra magic power!

# LEARNING
# GAMES

**W**herever and whenever I can, I try to make what we're doing into a learning game. Both my girls frequently accompany me when I travel for work and rather than take the journey for granted – just getting from A to B – I make it as engaging as I can, if only for my own sake. For example, while waiting for our luggage at the carousel in baggage reclaim, I ask Ava to count the bags or point out the ones that have been around the carousel once already. It's great for developing recognition skills, not to mention helpful for finding your own luggage!

I also try to introduce new words into the conversation, or help them to differentiate between words that sound the same but have different spellings and uses by encouraging the girls to put them into sentences or make up a story around them. We've talked about the differences between "witch" and "which", for example, and had loads of fun with "heebie-jeebies"! The benefits of playing word games should never be underestimated.

Memory games are always fun (particularly as I still suffer from "baby brain"), and they definitely help to reinforce language and vocabulary. One of our favourites is the shopping game, where you work through the alphabet: "I went to the shop and in my basket I put . . . an artichoke, a balloon, a caravan, a dolphin, an egg timer" and so on. Encouraging the girls to think on their feet and actually use their developing language skills has brought them on by leaps and bounds. Best of all, they genuinely love to test their memories – and mine!

As grown-ups, it's easy to forget that it's the little details that make games and learning so exciting and fresh. Children love to ask questions, and they soak up facts, stories and information so easily it's scary. Making games of everyday situations and experiences makes them more appealing, as well as easier to absorb and understand. Why shouldn't learning be fun?

*Myleene*
*x*

# PLASTIC CUPS

Who'd have thought that the humble plastic cup could provide the basis for a number of entertaining and truly educational games? They can be adapted easily for different age groups. You'll need lots of cups to hand for some of these activities but they are usually pretty cheap to buy.

## WHAT TO DO:

**STACKING:** Little ones might need a little practise until they get the hang of it. For the simplest tower, you'll need three cups at the base, two in the second tier and one on the top. For a higher tower, you'll need a bigger base. Try building on a circular, triangular or square base, and count out the cups as you stack them. See who can build the tallest tower before it collapses, or who can build the biggest tower within a certain time limit.

Paint the cups different colours or draw simple shapes on them to make them up into sets. You might have, for example, six red, six blue, six yellow and six green cups. If two of you are playing, allocate the sets between you - player 1 will only use coloured cups, player 2 only cups with numbers on them - and mix up all the cups in the centre. Then race to see who can sort out their cups from the pile and build their tower first.

**HIDE & SEEK:** This is a good memory game. Place a few small items (plastic toys or balls, for example) under upturned plastic cups and try to remember which item is under which cup. Or play a pairs memory game - place two of each item under different cups, move them around to mix them up, then take turns picking them up (one cup per turn), to see what is beneath. The trick is to pay attention and remember what item is under what cup. When you think you have spotted two cups hiding a pair you can pick them both up on your next turn to win a point, or lose one if you are wrong. Begin with three pairs under six cups and increase the number as you get more practised at the game.

**CRAZY PATTERNS:** This may sound very simple, but arranging plastic cups in a pattern encourages sequencing skills, which helps with reading and language development. Using different coloured cups, or different sets of cups, arrange them in a pattern, such as one red, two green, two yellow, one blue, and then ask your child to repeat the sequence. Or ask them to create their own sequences.

**ART ATTACK:** Create pictures with upturned cups. Try something simple like a happy face, and then let your creative juices flow. This is a truly addictive activity, both for adults and children. If you have a supply of coloured or painted cups so much the better, begin using just two colours then branch out with more.

# COUNTING RHYMES

Children learn through play and remember things best through repetition and happily counting rhymes tick both of these boxes. They also encourage numeracy and help with speech and language development. Reciting them in unison on long car journeys can also help to stave off the inevitable, "Are we nearly there yet?" moment, or to distract children when they are feeling out of sorts.

## CHOOK, CHOOK

Good morning, Mrs Hen
Chook, chook, chook
Good morning, Mrs Hen
Chook, chook, chook
Good morning, Mrs Hen
How many chickens have you got?
Farmer, I've got ten
Four of them are yellow
Four of them are brown
Two of them are speckled red
The finest in the town
Five of them go chirpy chirp

# ONE, TWO, BUCKLE MY SHOE

One, two, buckle my shoe
Three, four, open the door
Five, six, pick up sticks
Seven, eight, lay them straight
Nine, ten, a good fat hen
Eleven, twelve, dig and delve
Thirteen, fourteen, maids a-courting
Fifteen, sixteen, maids in the kitchen
Seventeen, eighteen, maids are waiting
Nineteen, twenty, my plate is empty

# ONE, TWO, THREE, FOUR, FIVE

One, two, three, four, five
Once I caught a fish alive
Six, seven, eight, nine, ten
Then I let it go again
Why did I let it go?
Because it bit my finger so
Which finger did it bite?
This little finger on the right

# FIVE CURRANT BUNS

Five currant buns in a baker's shop
Round and fat with a cherry on the top
Along came (say your child's name)
With a penny one day
Bought a currant bun and took it away

Four currant buns in a baker's shop
Round and fat with a cherry on the top
Along came (say your child's name)
With a penny one day
Bought a currant bun and took it away

Three currant buns in a baker's shop ...
(carry on for three, two, and then one currant bun)

No currant buns in a baker's shop
Round and fat with a cherry on the top
Along came (say your child's name)
With a penny one day
"I'm sorry", said the baker
"There are no buns today"

# FIVE LITTLE MONKEYS

Five little monkeys jumping on the bed
One fell off and bumped his head.
Mama called the doctor and the doctor said
"No more monkeys jumping on the bed!"

Four little monkeys jumping on the bed
One fell off and bumped his head
Mama called the doctor and the doctor said
"No more monkeys jumping on the bed!"

Three little monkeys jumping on the bed
One fell off and bumped his head
Mama called the doctor and the doctor said
"No more monkeys jumping on the bed!"

Two little monkeys jumping on the bed
One fell off and bumped his head
Mama called the doctor and the doctor said
"No more monkeys jumping on the bed!"

One little monkey jumping on the bed
He fell off and bumped his head
Mama called the doctor and the doctor said
"No more monkeys jumping on the bed!"

No little monkeys jumping on the bed
They're all jumping on the sofa instead!

# TEN IN THE BED

There were ten in the bed
And the little one said
"Roll over, roll over!"
So they all rolled over
And one fell out

There were nine in the bed
And the little one said
"Roll over, roll over!"
So they all rolled over
And one fell out

There were eight in the bed
And the little one said
"Roll over, roll over!"
So they all rolled over
And one fell out

There were seven in the bed
And the little one said,
"Roll over, roll over!"
So they all rolled over
And one fell out

There were six in the bed
And the little one said
"Roll over, roll over!"
So they all rolled over
And one fell out

There were five in the bed
And the little one said
"Roll over, roll over!"
So they all rolled over
And one fell out

There were four in the bed
And the little one said
"Roll over, roll over!"
So they all rolled over
And one fell out

There were three in the bed
And the little one said
"Roll over, roll over!"
So they all rolled over
And one fell out

There were two in the bed
And the little one said
"Roll over, roll over!"
So they all rolled over
And one fell out

There was one in the bed
And the little one said
"Roll over, roll over!"
So he rolled over
And he fell out

There were none in the bed
So no-one said
"Roll over, roll over!"

# FIVE LITTLE DUCKS

Five little ducks went swimming one day
Over the pond and far away
Mummy duck said, "Quack, quack, quack, quack"
But only four little ducks came back

Four little ducks went swimming one day
Over the pond and far away
Mummy duck said, "Quack, quack, quack, quack"
But only three little ducks came back

Three little ducks went swimming one day
Over the pond and far away
Mummy duck said, "Quack, quack, quack, quack"
But only two little ducks came back

Two little ducks went swimming one day
Over the pond and far away
Mummy duck said, "Quack, quack, quack, quack"
But only one little duck came back

One little duck went swimming one day
Over the pond and far away
Mummy duck said, "Quack, quack, quack, quack"
But no little ducks came swimming back
So Mummy duck said, "Quack, quack, quack, quack!"
And all her five little ducks came back

# 114

# SORTING GAMES

The basic activity of sorting helps children to learn about shape and colour and to categorise items. You can also use a sorting game as a way of getting children to tidy away toys and games at the end of the day!

## WHAT TO DO:

**COLOURS:** Make use of any items that you have around the home in a number of colours (balls, building blocks, etc.), and ask your child to sort them into colours. Tell them to arrange all the green books together on a shelf, and then red ones, and so on. Or ask them to sort the contents of their pencil and crayon box into colours, or to tip out the contents of the sock drawer and do the same – and while they're at it, they could sort them into pairs too!

**ANIMALS:** If you have a collection of small plastic animals, help your child to group them together in types. Put all the pigs together, then the cows, sheep, or pick out the farm animals from those that live at the zoo. Should snakes be put in a different category from ducks? If so, why? If you don't have enough toy animals, cut out pictures of animals from a magazine and ask your child to categorise them. Once they've mastered those, move on to fish, insects, birds, reptiles, etc.

**FOOD:** Draw or cut out pictures of different types of food, and ask your child to group them by type – vegetables, fruit, meat, fish and grains, for example. Then sort them according to meal type – breakfast, dinner and snack. Ask them to pick out pictures of their favourite food and arrange it into a meal on a paper plate. This game provides an opportunity to talk about nutrition, too.

**SHAPES:** Cut out different shapes from paper or card (circles, hearts, squares, stars and lots of other different shapes) and ask your child to group them together. When they've mastered the basic shapes, make it slightly more complicated by cutting some large and some small squares, circles, etc., so that your child must sort by two criteria: shape and size. Or colour the shapes or write numbers or letters on them, in order to introduce another level of choice. A jar of assorted pasta shapes from the kitchen cupboard will also do, if you're short on time.

# DOT-TO-DOT PICTURES

This is a creative way to use a tried and tested activity to help your child to practise their numbers as well as develop hand-eye co-ordination.

## WHAT TO DO:

Start by drawing basic shapes (circles, stars, hearts, etc.) very lightly in pencil on a sheet of paper. Using a felt-tip pen, ink in solid dots at intervals along the shape outline. Number each dot in sequence and rub out the pencil outline. Ask your child to complete the dot-to-dot picture, beginning at dot number one. Keep the shapes small or simple for young children so that you can keep the numbering below ten. After shapes, try simple images such as a sailboat or a house. Substitute letters for the numbers, again in sequence, to help your child practise the alphabet.

Once your child has got the idea, create dot-to-dot pictures of their favourite characters or themes (trucks, animals, and so on). Find a suitable image in a book or magazine and, placing a sheet of thin white paper or tracing paper over the top, trace over parts of the picture in the normal way, creating a line, but use the dot-to-dot and numbering system for other parts. Encourage your child to create their own pictures as well, helping them place theirs dots and numbers/letters. Now it's your turn to guess what they've drawn.

Use the method described above to write out simple words or your child's name in dot-to-dots. It's a good way for them to practise hand control and using a pencil. You can also write dot-to-dot thank you notes for your child to send to friends or grandparents. Or ask them want they want to say and write it out for them in dot-to-dot.

# 116

## JIGSAW PICTURES

Help develop your child's visual perception and fine motor skills by encouraging them to complete a drawing that you have begun.

### WHAT TO DO:

Start with simple shapes. Draw half a square, half a happy face or half a heart, and ask your child to complete it. Or try drawing an incomplete figure, with only one eye and one foot, for example, and ask them to fill in the missing parts. Or print out a picture of a favourite character, cut it in half, glue it to a sheet of paper and ask your little one to complete its mirror image. They will also learn about symmetry and opposites while having fun.

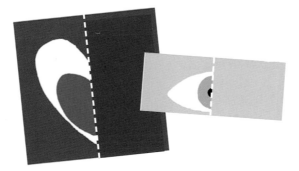

# FIND A LETTER,
# MAKE A WORD

These games help children with vocabulary and spelling, and to learn about the nature of competition as well. Use letter tiles from a word game, or make your own set using individual pieces of card.

## WHAT TO DO:

**MAKE A WORD:** This can be played with just two or in teams if you have a number of children. Pick out a few different words from the tiles. Choose just one or two words and keep them short for very young children, such as "dog" and "mat", while older children should be able to manage four or five longer words. Mix up the tiles and turn them face down in front of each player. If you don't have duplicates of the tiles, you will have to give each player different words, so make sure they are of the same difficulty level to keep things fair. At the word "Go!" players turn over their tiles and the race is on to start making words. Help younger children by giving them clues – it begins with "C", it lives on a farm and gives us milk . . .

**FIND THE WORD:** Ask your child to think of a word, "bus" for example. Then arrange six letter tiles in front of them, including "B", "U" and "S", but adding three others. Now ask your child to sound out the letters in "bus" and pick them out from the six tiles in front of them. If this proves a little difficult to begin with, ask them for their word, give them the letters for that word only, and ask them to point to the letters and sound them out. You could arrange the letters first in the right and then in the wrong order. Start with three-letter words and work your way up. Ask your little one to pick out their name and then their pet or teddy's name.

**ANAGRAMS:** Rearrange the letters of a chosen word and see if your child can find it, for example, "car" is hidden in "arc", and "milk" is hidden in "imkl" (you won't always be able to make a true anagram). Your child will have fun creating their own anagrams for you, too, although the word you have to find may not be spelled correctly!

**WEIRD WORDS:** See how many words you can make together from a stack of tiles. Make up silly words, too, and give them crazy meanings.

**LETTER HUNT:** If your child isn't quite ready for spelling, work on matching the tiles, pick out all the "B"s, for example. Then think of things in the house that begin with that letter (bottles, bins, beds, buckets, bananas).

# 118

# PICTURE BINGO

Make a picture bingo game based on one of your child's interests. Children learn matching and memory skills, and develop critical thinking and concentration, too. Two can play this game but one person has to double up as the caller (promising not to cheat) and check their own card.

## WHAT YOU'LL NEED:

- **Magazines or downloaded pictures**
- **Scissors**
- **Sheets of paper or card, A4 size**
- **Pen or pencil**
- **Ruler**
- **Bowl**
- **Tiddlywinks counters or buttons, for markers**

## WHAT TO DO:

Cut out lots of different pictures to suit your child's chosen theme, using magazines or downloaded images. If it's football you might choose a ball, goalpost, team shirt, referee's whistle, piece of grass (the pitch!), and so on. For Cinderella, choose a broom, shoe, prince, pumpkin, clock, etc. Each picture should be small enough to fit on an A4-size bingo card divided into four or six squares for young children or up to twelve squares for older children. You will need multiples of each picture depending on the number of players plus one for the bingo caller's bowl. The pictures don't have to be identical but should show the same item – you could also draw them rather than cut them out.

Now make the bingo cards. Paste the pictures onto the cards, one in each square. Each card must have the same set of pictures and each row must be identical. Place the remaining set of pictures in the bowl and mix them up. Give each player a set of markers (buttons or tiddlywinks counters), enough to cover all the squares on their card.

Ask the caller to dip their hand in the bowl and call out what is in the picture. Each player then places a marker on their bingo card in the appropriate place. The child who finishes either a line or the whole card first shouts "Bingo!" and wins the game. To introduce an element of chance, rather than just see who is the fastest to spot that a line is filled up, vary the position of the pictures on the cards (but each card still has the same set of pictures). For example, the top row of card 1 may have a ball, grass and a boot, whereas the top row of card 2 could have grass, a whistle and a ball. The winner is the first person to fill up a row.

Practise colour recognition by making a colour bingo card, or one with numbers and letters. If your child is working on learning basic words, play word bingo. Change things around a little by using sounds. For example use phonics in alphabet bingo - ask the caller to say the sound for "A" "B", etc., rather than the name of the letter, or the sounds that animals make (meow, quack, moo) for animal bingo.

# I SPY COLOURS

This is an old favourite for lots of children. This simple game will help young children to learn their colours and sounds.

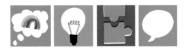

## WHAT TO DO:

Ask your child to look around and "spy" something coloured, "I spy something pink". You then have to guess what the "something" is. You can make the game a little more difficult by choosing more sophisticated colours such as turquoise and violet, or combinations of colours – pink and mint-green, pale blue with peach stripes. The (blue) sky's pretty much the limit with this game.

Now, try moving onto sounds. There are approximately 44 phonic sounds in the English language, made up from the 26 letters of the alphabet, that children learn in order to spell, read and write. Developing an ear for these sounds will definitely give them a head start when it comes to literacy. Make sure you use the sound rather than the name of the letter, as most children now learn phonetically and letter names are learned only later on. It goes without saying that I Spy is a fantastic game for car journeys.

# 120

# FLAGS OF THE WORLD

Children love to test their memory skills. Learning to recognise the flags of the world will test their knowledge on several levels, from colours, shapes and designs to fun facts about different countries.

## WHAT TO DO:

Which three flags make up the flag for the United Kingdom? What does the cross on the English flag stand for and why does the Welsh flag have a dragon? What are the stars on the United States flag, and what do the coloured stripes on the French, German and Spanish flags represent? Unless you are a whiz at flags yourself, you'll probably need a book or the Internet to help you out on this activity. See if you can learn two or three new flags every day, and then test each other to see what you can remember about them the following day.

Ask your child to draw and colour their favourite flags. Play flag bingo or buy a flag sticker book to reinforce their knowledge. Make a flag scrapbook together, and group all the European flags on one page and the African on another and label them, or pick out all the flags with stars on them. Or why not try making a collage using different flags?

# GLOBE GAMES

These games teach children about the world and are bound to send you off on lots of interesting detours, talking about ways to travel, geography and cultural differences between countries and peoples. Having travelled with me to so many places, my girls love anything to do with maps and are always planning our next destination.

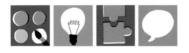

## WHAT TO DO:

**WHERE AM I?:** Learning to find their way around a map is an important skill to master. Ask your child to point out their country on a map of the world. Can they find their region, then town or village? Or their street on a map of your locality? Where is their country? What would they need to do to reach another part of the world – cross a river, a mountain range, a whole continent, the ocean? Ask your child to find where they were born, and where their grandparents were born. Was it in the same country? Where have they travelled on holiday?

**WHERE WILL I FIND . . .?:** This is a great game for learning about different cultures. For example, where will I find the didgeridoo? Where will I find the Eiffel Tower, a flamenco dancer, rattlesnakes, maple syrup, or the pyramids? Ask your child to point them out on a map. Then ask them to make up questions for you. Linking pieces of knowledge (in this case, a place and information about it) is an effective tool for development and makes the most of children's natural curiosity, inspiring an interest in learning.

**WORLD A–Z:** See how many countries, cities, seas or rivers, islands, or anything else geographical, that you can find that start with the letter "a". Move on to "b" and work your way through the alphabet. If your child isn't reading yet, see if they can think of a place beginning with each letter – they may be aware of Ireland, for example, or England, Australia, or Canada, then help them to find it in an atlas.

# LOOK IT UP!

We often try to direct our children's learning rather than give them free rein to find out about whatever interests them. This activity is about finding out things and making the most of children's natural curiosity about the world.

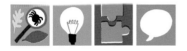

WHAT TO DO:

Ask your child what they would like to know more about and see where it takes you both. Would they like to know about the moon? Or pigs? Have they ever wondered how paper is made? Or why the leaves change colour in autumn? How tall they might be when they grow up? For young children learning is a fairly natural process - the proverbial "little sponges" soak up information all day long. If they ask questions that you can't answer on the spot, make a note and return to them later when you can research them together.

Develop projects that you can do together based on your child's interest in a topic, such as finding out more about a country that sparked their curiosity in the Globe game opposite. Again, let their questions guide their learning.

You may not end up learning about the traditional matters like culture, population, religion or capital cities, but knowledge of any description is worth accumulating.

# HAPPY FACE, SAD FACE

There are a number of variations on this activity based on the human face, which is one of the first recognisable images that children draw. They are designed to help with emotional development and imagination.

Help your child to draw a variety of faces showing different emotions on paper plates or card circles – happy, sad, frightened, excited, bored, etc. You can use the results in a number of ways below.

## WHAT TO DO:

**WHAT MAKES YOU FEEL LIKE THAT?:** Ask your child to hold up one of the faces and explain what might make them feel that way. What makes them frightened? Or sad? This activity will help little ones understand the concept of feelings and how different things make us feel different ways, which is important for developing empathy for others.

**THEY'RE FEELING:** Read a favourite book and have the faces to hand. As the story progresses, ask your child to hold up a face to show what the characters are feeling. The faces will probably pop up and down at a dramatic rate.

**TELL ME A STORY:** Hold up a face for your child and ask them to begin a story about someone who is feeling the emotion shown on the face. Ask them to invent a character and explain what happened to produce that emotion. Now hold up a different face with a change of emotion and see if your child can develop the story to explain why their character is now feeling sad, angry, etc. This is a great tool for language development and problem-solving, not to mention emotional intelligence. And, of course, it's also fun!

# 124

# GO FISH

Most of us will be aware of this simple game, which helps children practise matching skills and develop memory, speech and language. If you don't have a deck of playing cards, make your own by drawing or pasting pictures and/or letters and numbers on squares of card. All you need is two of each card and enough cards to make the game last for a reasonable length of time – say around forty cards in total.

WHAT TO DO:
Shuffle the pack and deal five cards to each player. If only two are playing, you may wish to leave some of the cards out of a conventional pack of fifty-two. Place the remaining cards face down in a pile between you. Players should hold their cards so that they can see them, but no one else can. Players should look at their cards and place face down any pairs they already have in their hand. Then, moving around the circle, player 1 asks the player to their left, player 2, "Do you have a . . . (three/blue circle/cat)?" depending on the deck of cards.

If player 2 has the matching card, it must be handed over to make a pair. Player 1 then places the pair face down in front of them. If player 2 does not have the card, they say "Go fish!" and player 1 picks up a card from the pile in the middle. If the new card makes a pair, player 1 places the pair face down in front of them and has another turn. If not, they keep the card with the others in their hand and their turn ends. Player 2 then asks player 3 for a matching card, and so on. If a player runs out of cards, they must collect five more from the pile. The player who has the most pairs is the winner.

# LOOK HOW BIG I AM

Make your own height chart. Measuring is a skill that helps to encourage numeracy, but what will really interest your child with this activity is that it touches on something that obsesses most children: how big they are getting and how quickly!

## WHAT YOU'LL NEED:

- **Large sheet of card, cut in 2 or 3 pieces lengthways so that when joined it makes a strip approx. 1.5m long x 15cm wide**
- **Craft glue or sticky tape**
- **2 x 1-metre paper measuring tape (you can often get these free of charge in furniture shops)**
- **Felt-tip pens, stickers, pictures cut from magazines, and anything else to decorate with**

## WHAT TO DO:

Join together the pieces of card with sticky tape or glue to make one long strip. Glue one of the measuring tapes along the side of the card, making sure that the top end is flush with the top of the strip. Glue the second tape immediately below the first, and cut off any excess at the bottom. Now change the numbers on the second tape to run consecutively on from the end of the first, so change 1cm to 101cm, 2cm to 102cm, etc. Ask your little one to count the centimetres while you do the writing, or vice versa.

Fun ideas to decorate the chart include drawing something tall down the length of it, like a giraffe. Now fasten it to a door or a wall, making sure the bottom of the chart is flush with the floor. Add a photo at the appropriate height of your child on each birthday, or take a photo each time your child is measured. Or draw something that is about the same height as your child beside the relevant height mark. For example, if they've just reached 60cm you might draw a monkey and a penguin when they get to 80cm. Have fun looking up creatures that are the same height as your child.

# 126

# CAR GAMES

Many games and activities in this book can be adapted for use while travelling, and it's good to know that keeping children occupied can also stretch their minds and aid their development.

**ALPHABET GAME:** The game is to cross out each letter as soon as they see it written in a word somewhere on the journey. They need to keep their eyes open for signs, destinations on the front of a bus, and so on. The first one to cross out all their letters is the winner. This game works best in built-up areas, although car number plates are a good source of letters.

**CAR BINGO:** Cut out or draw pictures of all the things you are likely to see on your journey – a lamppost, a white van, a set of traffic lights, a dog . . . and paste them onto a sheet of card. Prepare a card with the same pictures for each child so they can play against each other, or give them a different one each. The first child to spot and cross off all the items pictured is the winner. For long journeys, you might need to prepare several different cards to keep everyone busy.

**GUESS MY WORD:** One person thinks of a word (an animal, a fruit or vegetable, a favourite character from TV or a book). The others take turns asking questions such as, "Is it red?", "Does it run?", "Can you eat it?" until the correct word is guessed. You can only ask questions requiring the answer "yes" or "no". The player who guesses correctly is the next one to think of a word. For younger children, you may want to narrow it down to a specific category, such as fruit.

**THE MEMORY GAME:** Use the things you see on the journey, taking turns to go through the letters of the alphabet. For example, player 1 spots an airplane and says "A is for airplane", player 2 sees a bag and says "A is for airplane, B is for bag", player 3 looks around until they notice a catseye and say "A is for airplane, B is for bag, C is for catseye". The person who gets the furthest without forgetting an item wins.

# WORD GAMES

Playing with words and sounds is one of the best ways to encourage a broad vocabulary and linguistic skills. Whether trying to master tongue twisters or create silly words of their own, it helps children to improve pronunciation and enunciation and provides plenty of fun at the same time.

# TONGUE TWISTERS:

You are as likely to struggle with these as your children,
so be prepared for a little healthy competition!
Here are some of my favourites:

Which wristwatches are Swiss wristwatches?

How much wood would a woodchuck chuck if
a woodchuck could chuck wood?
He would chuck, he would, as much as he could, and chuck as
much as a woodchuck would, if a woodchuck could chuck wood.

Peter Piper picked a peck of pickled peppers
Did Peter Piper pick a peck of pickled peppers?
If Peter Piper picked a peck of pickled peppers
Where's the peck of pickled peppers Peter Piper picked?

She sells seashells by the seashore.

Who knew you knew Sue?
Sue knew you knew Sue.

A big bug bit the little beetle but the little beetle bit the big bug back.

Red lorry, yellow lorry.

If there's a phrase that you find yourself stumbling over, add it to
your tongue twister collection and see if anyone else fares better!

# RHYMING GAMES:

Teaching children to use rhyme is a lovely way of encouraging early reading. There is much research to suggest that children find it easier to pick out the phonic sounds in rhyming words and also to spell them. Look at a book of rhyme together and point out and say aloud the rhyming words. Explain to your child that these are words that sound alike but are not the same. Easy examples are simple, one-syllable words such as cat, mat, fat and pat. In longer words it is usually the last part of the word that rhymes (mother/another, packet/racquet). Some of my favourite books (see page 15), such as those by Julia Donaldson or Dr. Seuss are perfect for this activity.

Choose a word and take turns to think of a rhyme until no one can go any further. The last person to think of a rhyme wins. Practise using rhyme by creating your own rhyming sentences. For example, "The little teddy bear was brown" could be followed by, "And on his face he wore a frown". Give very young budding poets the second sentence minus the final word and see what they can come up with.

Or why not make up a story, word by word? The first player begins with their word, which might be "One". The next player adds another (perhaps "day"), the next player adds their word, and so on. Since each player may only contribute one word at a time, all kinds of weird and wonderful stories result, usually accompanied by much giggling.

# MEMORY GAMES:

On page 24, 170 and 195, I explained a few of the memory games that I enjoy playing with the girls, and there are dozens like these.

The suitcase is a good one and conjures up some bizarre images as you imagine cramming all sorts of unlikely items into a suitcase. Choose different items beginning with each letter of the alphabet in succession, "I packed my suitcase with an apple". The next person repeats this and adds their item, "I packed my suitcase with an apple and a balloon, the third person "I packed my suitcase with an apple, a balloon and a candle". You'll be getting the idea by now. Carry on all the way up to zebra or zither if you can. Make it harder by using an adjective, "an amber apple, a blue balloon, a creepy candle, a delicate dragon . . ."

# Numbers and sounds

Playing with numbers and sounds is educational and fun for your children, while also making them comfortable and familiar with the concepts of language and numeracy. Try to incorporate them into daily life as much as possible.

Count your way up the stairs, count each small finger as it goes into a glove, count strokes as you brush hair, and "time" your children by counting as they go about various tasks. Ask them to time you, too, on a trip to the loo or a telephone call. Ask them to choose four apples and two oranges at the supermarket, and then work out how many pieces of fruit they have in total. Play shop and help them to work out the change from purchases, but keep it simple at the outset. Let them buy their own small things at the shops and ask them in advance to check if they have enough money and what kind of change they can expect. Although this all sounds pretty obvious, it can give children a massive head start when it comes to working with numbers on their own.

Language is another area that can be explored with great success. Make up silly rhymes together, tell stories to one another, and guess the missing word in a sentence (see page 198). Take time to point out letter sounds or phonics whenever you can. These days, most children are taught to read and spell phonetically, so when spelling out words or playing language games, use sounds rather than the names of letters whenever possible. When playing I Spy, ask your child to spell out everyday items in sounds, such as their clothes as they get dressed. Look at the letters of short words in books or magazines and sound them out together. Ask them what their favourite animal beginning with "buh" is, or their favourite "tuh" food. It doesn't need to be turned into a lesson; just in the form of playful chatter that draws their attention to words and spellings and the way they sound.

It goes without saying that reading to your children is probably the single most important way of encouraging literacy and a love of words, but don't rule out some of the hugely exciting online games and programmes that help make spelling and phonics easy and engaging. With supervision (a laptop or a tablet set up in the kitchen while you cook), your child can learn and be entertained at the same time.

# IN THE KITCHEN

**A**nyone who knows me will also know that I cannot cook. No really, not a thing. I'm an expert "warmer upper", but the art of cooking utterly mystifies me, and even more so simply for pleasure. Paradoxically, I am also completely obsessive about my children's diets and very eager for them to have fresh, healthy meals every day.

While what I know about nutrition may not be reflected in my ability actually to cook, I am supremely aware that what my girls eat is the foundation of their health both now and in the future. As a result, my girls now know that it is good for them to "eat a rainbow" and that they should fill their plates with colour from a variety of different food groups. They are pretty adventurous when it does come to eating, which is a blessing. I couldn't afford for them not to be, as my work takes me (and therefore them) to so many different and random places. Looking for pasta in Costa Rica, for example, was never an option, and they just had to muck in and eat what everyone else was eating, which in this case was shellfish, tropical fruit and huevos rancheros!

I truly believe that spending time with your children in the kitchen encourages them to eat well, experiment with different tastes and textures, and develop a happy, healthy relationship with food. No matter how unconfident or bad at cooking, or busy you may be, everyone can produce a few "winning" dishes, even if it does mean a fair bit of experimentation along the way. So whether you are a Nigella or a Myleene, it's great to show your children what goes into food, what effect it has on their body, how things taste and feel, as well as to experience the simple pleasures of kneading bread or whisking egg whites.

Across the years I've built up a good store of recipes that I have managed to master, and I've noted them down here. Most are simple (a few are not so simple, but chances are that you are more accomplished in the kitchen than I am) and all of them can be created with even the littlest fingers. So have fun, make a mess and enjoy the time you spend in the kitchen together.

*Myleene*
*x*

# HOME-MADE BUTTER

This recipe gives children an insight into the churning process that makes the butter we buy in the shops. Use the milk that is created in the process (buttermilk) for yummy American-style pancakes or muffins. It's lighter and less calorific than regular milk but still contains lots of calcium for young bones and teeth.

MAKES: 1 small jar

INGREDIENTS:
- 400ml double cream
- Pinch of salt, if desired

WHAT TO DO:
You'll need several clean, dry jars with lids. If more than one child is cooking with you, it's fun for each to have their own jar. Half fill each jar with double cream. If your family is used to salted butter, add a pinch of salt at this stage. Screw on the lids tightly and shake the jars up and down with all your might until the cream thickens and begins to form a lump, just like it does when you whip it with beaters. It can take 10 minutes of vigorous shaking, so take turns when little arms get tired. It won't hamper the process if you need to take a break from time to time.

When the cream has turned into yellowish curds surrounded by liquid, strain off the liquid – the buttermilk – into another bowl or jar, and place the curds in a strainer. Run under cold water for 3-4 minutes to remove any small bits of curd and then, with the water still running, use your hand to press the curd together to form a lovely round ball or small log. It may look a little whiter than the butter you buy in the supermarket, and if you haven't used salt, it may also taste different, but believe me, the freshness of this butter is unbeatable.

# CHEESY BREADSTICKS

These breadsticks are a super-quick snack that can be made easily by little hands. They can be stored in an airtight container for up to a week.

MAKES: **24**

INGREDIENTS:
- **Plain flour, for rolling**
- **350g packet of ready-rolled puff pastry**
- **8 tbsp Parmesan cheese**
- **Freshly ground black pepper, to taste**
- **1 tsp paprika**

WHAT TO DO:
Preheat the oven to 220°C/Gas 7.

Grease two baking sheets or trays with a little butter, or line them with greaseproof paper and place to one side.

On a lightly floured surface or cutting board unfold the puff pastry. Sprinkle it evenly with 6 tbsp of Parmesan cheese and a little black pepper. Fold the pastry over and use a rolling pin to roll it out until it is about 25mm thick. Sprinkle with the remaining Parmesan and the paprika, and cut it into strips about 50mm wide. Place the strips on the baking sheets, leaving some space between them. Bake in the preheated oven for 12 minutes or until they are a lovely, golden brown colour. Remove from the oven, cool slightly and serve.

# TRAFFIC LIGHT SANDWICHES

It's amazing what children will eat in a sandwich if it looks enticing. Many little ones will baulk at the idea of tomatoes or lettuce but when sandwiches are presented as traffic lights, they'll gobble them up.

MAKES: **2**

INGREDIENTS:
- **4 slices of wholegrain bread**
- **2 tbsp hummus (or 2 slices of ham/mild Cheddar cheese)**
- **2 tsp unsalted butter**
- **4 tbsp shredded lettuce**
- **4 tbsp grated carrot**
- **4 cherry tomatoes, halved**

WHAT TO DO:
Use an apple corer or a small round cookie cutter to cut out two parallel columns of three circles on two slices of bread. Each slice should have six circles or two sets of traffic lights.

Spread the remaining two pieces of bread with butter or margarine and top both with hummus, ham or cheese. Place a row of shredded lettuce on the bottom third of one of the slices (on top of the ham or cheese) and a row of grated carrot above that. Carefully place one of the bread slices with holes on top. To finish the sandwich, place a half cherry tomato inside each of the two top holes. You should be able to see the amber (carrot) and green (lettuce) lights beneath the red. Cut the sandwich in half to create two sets of traffic lights. Repeat to make the second sandwich. Ready, steady, chomp!

# BAKED POTATO BOATS

Decorating food may be time-consuming, but if a dish (or an unfamiliar ingredient) looks fun, children are much more likely to try it. You can make these into a meal by stirring a drained tin of tuna into the mashed flesh of the potatoes before they are returned to their "boats".

MAKES: **4**

INGREDIENTS:

- **2 large baking potatoes (such as Maris Piper or King Edward)**
- **1 small celery stick, very finely chopped**
- **1 small carrot, peeled and very finely chopped**
- **2 tbsp crème fraîche**
- **Salt and freshly ground black pepper, to taste**
- **Small tin of tuna or salmon (optional)**
- **75g Cheddar cheese, grated**
- **4 cocktail sticks**
- **2 slices of Red Leicester cheese or 2 square slices of roasted ham**

WHAT TO DO:
Preheat the oven to 200°C/Gas 6.

Wash the potatoes well, dry them and prick them several times with a fork (kids love doing this bit!). Place them on a baking tray and bake for 50 minutes, depending on the size of the potato, or until soft to the touch.

Remove from the oven and set to one side to cool slightly. Cut the potatoes in half and carefully scoop out the insides. Place in a bowl and mash until smooth.

Stir in the celery, carrot and crème fraîche, and season to taste. If you are adding tuna (or even drained, tinned salmon), now's the time. Return the potato mixture to the potato shells and top with grated cheese. Place the potato boats back in the oven for 10-12 minutes, or until the cheese is melted, golden and bubbly.

Place a boat on each plate. Cut the cheese or ham slices in half diagonally, and carefully thread each one onto a cocktail stick to create a sail. Pop one onto the top of each boat and serve.

# ROASTED CORN ON THE COB

It's not always easy to get children to eat vegetables, but I know that if they have made a dish themselves, they are more likely to eat it. This is a winner every time.

MAKES: **24**

INGREDIENTS:
- **4 corn cobs (as fresh as possible)**
- **25g butter**
- **Salt and freshly ground black pepper, to taste**

WHAT TO DO:
Preheat the oven to 220°C/Gas 7.

Remove the husk and silks from the corn (if necessary). Rub the ears with a little butter and sprinkle with salt and pepper. Wrap the ears in aluminium foil, place on a rack in the oven and roast for 20 minutes. Bigger ears may need a further 10 minutes. Open up the foil packets and stab the ears with a fork to see if they are tender, before removing them from the oven. Allow to cool slightly before removing from the foil and serving, with fanfare and a flourish!

# MINI ME PIZZAS

The best part of these mini pizzas is making the faces. Encourage children to use some of the many possible ingredients to create portraits of their own faces, and for extra laughs, yours! Mix and match the suggestions below, raw or cooked.

MAKES: **6**

INGREDIENTS:
- **3 English muffins (plain or wholegrain), halved**
- **6 tbsp pasta sauce (or tomato**
- **purée)**
- **200g mozzarella cheese, grated**

FOR EYES: **Black or green olives (de-stoned; green olives stuffed with pimento make particularly creepy eyes), baby carrots (peeled and cut into rounds or grated), miniature pepperoni (cut into rounds), peas (frozen), cherry tomatoes (halved)**

FOR NOSES: **Mushrooms (sliced), cauliflower or broccoli florets (steamed), cooked ham (sliced or minced), onions (finely chopped)**

FOR HAIR: **Spinach (sliced), sweetcorn (tinned), mince (cooked), asparagus spears, onions (sliced), pineapple (chopped)**

FOR MOUTHS: **Green beans (steamed), cherry tomatoes (quartered), sweet pepper (in strips), cooked ham or chicken (sliced)**

WHAT TO DO:
Preheat the oven to 180°C/Gas 4.

Place the English muffins cut side up on a baking sheet. Pop into the oven for 5 minutes and then remove. Spread the pizza or pasta sauce or tomato purée over the top and sprinkle with mozzarella cheese. Work can now begin on the portraits.

Give each child two muffin halves and ask them to create their own face with the food. Offer plenty of different toppings to encourage creativity (not to mention the possibility of slipping in a few more nutrients).

When the portraits are complete, return the decorated muffins to the oven for 10-15 minutes or until the cheese has melted and is slightly browned.

# SNOWFLAKE TORTILLAS

These beautiful snowflakes appeal to eyes and tummies!
Use wholemeal or corn tortillas for extra fibre and nutrients.

MAKES: **6**

INGREDIENTS:
- **6 large tortillas**
- **2 tbsp vegetable oil**
- **4 tbsp icing sugar**
- **2 tsp edible glitter**

WHAT TO DO:
Preheat the oven to 180°C/Gas 4.

Warm the tortillas in the microwave for 10 seconds to make them more pliable. Fold each one in half and then in half again so that it resembles a wedge of a pie. Now cut shapes into the tortillas, as if you were making a paper snowflake. Snip into the folded edges to create a scalloped edge. Place the folded tortilla on a flat surface and using a knife, cut out small shapes (triangles, diamonds, hearts) from the centre of it – be careful not to cut across the whole width of the tortilla or the snowflake will fall apart when unfolded. Finally, cut a small round from the folded point.

Open up the tortillas and lay them flat on baking sheets. You should have pretty snowflake patterns. Brush each with vegetable oil and place in the oven for about 5 minutes, or until the snowflakes are slightly crisp. While they are still warm, sift icing sugar over the surface and then sprinkle with some edible glitter. Serve warm.

**135**

# CHOCOLATE CHIP COOKIES

I promise you that these are the very best fat, chewy, yummy chocolate chip cookies on the face of the earth and even I can make them! The girls love pouring ingredients into the bowl and stirring them up. For an occasional sugary feast, we adorn them with Smarties® or M&Ms®, which can be placed on the top about halfway through cooking.

**MAKES: 18-24**

**INGREDIENTS:**
- **175g unsalted butter**
- **200g dark brown sugar**
- **100g caster sugar**
- **1 tsp vanilla extract**
- **1 large egg, plus 1 large egg yolk**
- **250g plain flour**
- **½ tsp bicarbonate of soda**
- **½ tsp baking powder**
- **½ tsp salt**
- **350g dark chocolate chips**

WHAT TO DO:
Preheat the oven to 180°C/Gas 4. Prepare a couple of baking trays by greasing with a little butter or vegetable fat, or lining them with silicone or parchment.

To make the cookie dough, in a medium mixing bowl cream together the butter and both sugars until light and fluffy. Beat in the vanilla and eggs until well combined and aerated. Sift the flour, bicarbonate of soda, baking powder and salt, and then stir in, slowly and carefully, until just blended. Stir in the chocolate chips with a wooden spoon until just combined.

Drop the cookie dough onto the prepared baking trays, using around 1-2 tbsp of dough for each one. You should end up with 18-24 large cookies. Place them on the trays around 3-4cm apart to allow for expansion in baking. Do not flatten them.

Bake in the preheated oven for about 15 minutes or until the cookies are nicely browned. Remove from the oven and cool for about 5 minutes, before placing on wire racks. The cookies should be chewy and moist, not too firm, and are nicest served just warm.

# FRUITY YOGHURT POPS

These fun pops are simple, nutritious and you don't even need moulds. What could be nicer?

**MAKES: 6**

**INGREDIENTS:**
- 2 small ripe bananas, peeled and cut into chunks
- 150g strawberries, washed and hulled
- 100g blueberries, washed
- 500ml plain or vanilla yoghurt
- 2 tbsp honey

**WHAT TO DO:**
Place all the ingredients in the bowl of a food processor or blender. Whiz on a low setting until the mixture is nice and smooth. Pour into six paper or plastic cups and place in the freezer for about 20 minutes. Remove from the freezer and gently poke a lolly stick or a wooden ice-cream spoon into the centre of each and return to the freezer for about 3 hours, or until frozen solid.

When you are ready to serve, dip each cup in a little warm water first to release it and distribute the pops to excited children (or adults). If you don't have any lolly sticks or spoons, turn the pops out into a bowl and top with some fresh fruit.

# FRUIT KEBABS

These kebabs are perfect for picnics, lunchboxes, parties, after-school snacks or dessert.

MAKES: **As many as you want**

INGREDIENTS:
- Kiwis, peeled and sliced
- Bananas, peeled and cut into rounds
- Strawberries, washed and hulled
- Grapes, washed (seedless are best)
- Raspberries, rinsed (firm ones are best)
- Oranges, peeled, de-seeded and cut into segments
- Apples, peeled, de-seeded and cut into chunks
- Mango, peeled, halved, de-stoned and cut into chunks
- Papaya, peeled, de-seeded and cut into chunks
- Melon, peeled, de-seeded and cut into chunks
- Dash of lemon juice
- ¼ tsp sugar or maple syrup
- Wooden skewers or lolly sticks

WHAT TO DO:
Thread small chunks of the prepared fruit into wooden skewers, brush with lemon juice and sugar or maple syrup (to prevent browning) and serve. If you are worried about the sharp ends of wooden skewers, snip them off before serving, or use lolly sticks.

For an extra special treat, blend a few squares of melted milk chocolate with 1 tbsp of cream to make a chocolatey dip.

# RAINBOW CAKE

This is one of those special occasion cakes that takes oodles of time to make but is definitely worth the effort. Children will love the dramatic look of the finished product, a rainbow of sponge cakes glued together beneath a delicious cream cheese frosting. They'll also learn about what secondary colours emerge when primary colours are mixed together.

SERVES: **12-14**

INGREDIENTS:
FOR THE CAKE:
- 350g unsalted butter, at room temperature, plus 25g for greasing
- 350g caster sugar or light brown sugar
- 6 large eggs
- 350g self-raising flour
- 1 tbsp vanilla extract
- 30ml semi-skimmed milk
- Red, blue and yellow food colour paste or gel

FOR THE FROSTING:
- 150g unsalted butter, softened
- 250g full fat cream cheese, at room temperature
- 1½ tsp vanilla extract
- 600g icing sugar, sifted
- Multicoloured Smarties® or sprinkles, to decorate (optional)

SPECIAL EQUIPMENT:
- 6 disposable aluminium foil sponge (or flan) tins, approx. 20cm
- 6 mixing bowls, medium size

## WHAT TO DO:

Preheat the oven to 180°C/Gas 4. To make the cake, cream together the butter and sugar in a large mixing bowl until light and fluffy, making sure there are no lumps. Add one of the eggs and combine with the butter and sugar, then add about a spoonful of the flour and combine. Make sure the egg and flour are well blended before adding another egg. Add more flour and continue alternating the two until all the eggs and flour have been used. Continue beating until the mixture is smooth, then stir in the vanilla extract. If the batter seems too thick, add up to 30ml of the milk, a teaspoon at a time. The batter should be smooth.

Divide the batter equally between the six mixing bowls. In the first bowl, add some red food colour paste or gel, a tiny bit at a time, and mix until the batter turns a good, deep red colour. In the second, add half the amount of red and a similar quantity of yellow to create a vibrant orange. Add just yellow to the third; in the fourth mix yellow and blue to make a nice deep green; make the batter plain blue in the fifth; and mix equal quantities of blue and red in the sixth to produce a lovely rich violet or indigo. If you're thinking that this sounds quite messy and fussy so far, it is, but I can guarantee that the results will be worth it.

Grease the six foil tins (or metal, if using) with a little butter and fill each with a different coloured batter, one colour per tin, leaving room for the cakes to rise, (approximately the space of your thumbnail),

Bake them in the preheated oven for around 20 minutes, or until a skewer placed in the centre comes out clean and the top springs back nicely to the touch. Remove from the oven and allow the sponges to cool in the tins for 10 minutes, then tip out onto a wire rack (the rack from a grill pan is a good substitute, if you don't have one). While they cool, you can make the frosting. Blend together the butter and cream cheese until smooth and fluffy. Stir in the vanilla extract (taste and add a little more if you like the vanilla flavour) and then beat in the sifted icing sugar, a little at a time. Continue beating until everything is blended and the frosting has a good, spreadable consistency.

Once the sponges are cool, it's time to assemble the cake. Start with the violet/indigo layer at the bottom, and cover the top and sides with a very thin layer of frosting (this is known as "crumb coating"). Next add the plain blue layer, and repeat the thin frosting. Now, move on to the green, yellow, orange and finally the red layer, repeating the same process. Place the cake in the refrigerator for about 30 minutes, then remove and, using a palette knife, cover the whole cake from top to bottom with a generous layer of frosting. Smooth it out neatly or go for a rough finish.

The beauty is in the cutting, when the beautiful layers of rainbow-coloured sponge are finally revealed! Decorate with brightly coloured Smarties® or sprinkles if you like, and serve with pride.

# APRICOT COOKIES

These chewy cookies are very simple to make and children love them. You can add sultanas or any other dried, chopped fruit, in place of apricots, if desired.

MAKES: **24**

INGREDIENTS:
- **150g unsalted butter, chopped into small pieces**
- **125g caster sugar**
- **100g rolled porridge oats**
- **100g self-raising flour**
- **150g dried apricots, chopped**
- **1 large egg, lightly beaten**
- **1 tbsp milk, if necessary**

WHAT TO DO:
Preheat the oven to 180°C/Gas 4.

Grease a baking tray or sheet with a little butter. Melt the butter and dissolve the sugar in a medium saucepan over medium heat, stirring frequently. Remove from the heat, pour the mixture into a large bowl and stir in the remaining ingredients. The mixture should be firm enough to drop onto a baking tray in teaspoon-sized balls. If it's too firm, add a little milk.

Spoon the mixture onto the tray a heaped teaspoon at a time, leaving about 2cm between each. Bake in the preheated oven for about 12 minutes or until the top of the cookies are a lovely, golden colour. Remove from the oven, allow to cool for a few minutes on the baking tray and then transfer to a wire rack to cool completely.

# STRAWBERRY FAIRIES

These little cupcakes are a twist on the traditional "butterfly" cakes. Filled with jam and a little whipped cream, they are topped with a strawberry body and cake "wings". Dust with icing sugar and a little edible glitter to finish them off.

MAKES: 12

INGREDIENTS:
- 125g unsalted butter, at room temperature
- 125g caster sugar
- 1 tsp vanilla extract
- 2 large eggs, lightly beaten
- 225g self-raising flour, sifted
- 150ml milk
- 3 tbsp strawberry jam
- 150ml double cream, lightly whipped
- 1 tbsp icing sugar
- 12 plump strawberries, rinsed and hulled
- Icing sugar and/or edible glitter, to dust

WHAT TO DO:
Preheat the oven to 180°C/Gas 4. Grease or line a 12-cup muffin/cupcake tin with cake cases and place to one side. Using a mixer or an electric whisk, cream together the butter, sugar and vanilla, and then beat in the eggs, one by one. Add half the flour and milk, continue to beat, then add the remainder of the flour and milk and incorporate until the batter is light and fluffy. Spoon the mixture into the cake cases.

Bake for about 20 minutes or until the cakes have risen nicely and are a soft golden brown – they should just spring back to the touch. Allow to cool slightly, then transfer to a wire rack. When the cakes are cool, carefully slice off the tops and scoop out a small circle of cake from the middle of each one. Cut each sliced top in half and place to one side. These will form the "wings". Fill the cavity with a little jam. Mix together the lightly whipped cream and icing sugar in a small mixing bowl and place a dollop over the jam-filled centres of the cakes.

Place a strawberry, the base uppermost, on top of the cream. This is the fairy body. Place a "wing" on each side and add a small blob of jam on the top of each strawberry for a head. Dust with icing sugar and/or glitter and serve daintily, like a fairy.

# RICE KRISPIE® TEDDIES

These are not only Myleene-friendly but also delicious! If you have nut allergies in your family, leave out the peanut butter and just add an extra handful of marshmallows and an extra tablespoon of butter. Make sure you grease your hands before attempting to mould the teddies.

**MAKES: 6-8 teddies**

**INGREDIENTS:**
- **50g unsalted butter**
- **50g smooth peanut butter**
- **1 tsp vanilla extract**
- **200g miniature marshmallows**
- **100g Rice Krispies®**
- **Chocolate buttons and sweets, to decorate**

**WHAT TO DO:**
Melt the butter and peanut butter together in the microwave in a microwave-safe bowl for 30-40 seconds, or in a small saucepan over medium heat for several minutes, or until smooth.

Remove from the heat, stir in the vanilla extract and add the marshmallows, continuing to stir until the marshmallows have melted. You may need to return the pan to the heat (or the bowl to the microwave) for a few moments to ensure the marshmallows are fully melted.

In a large bowl, combine the peanut butter mix and Rice Krispies® and stir until well coated. Place in the refrigerator for 5-10 minutes (no longer), then divide the mixture into 6-8 even sized balls. If the mixture is still too wet to mould, stir in a little icing sugar or refrigerate for a further 5 minutes.

Grease your hands (and those of your little helpers) with a little butter or olive/sunflower oil and mould one ball into a teddy's head or two to form a whole teddy. Place on a sheet of greaseproof paper.

Use chocolate buttons to make ears, a black or brown Smarties® (or other sweet) to create a nose, and use sweets or small dabs of writing icing for eyes.

Refrigerate until cool and then serve your teddies. You can use this mixture to create any shape you like. Rice Krispie® snakes are easy for little hands to make, or dip balls of the mixture into melted butter and then dust with icing sugar and/or desiccated coconut to make lovely Christmas baubles. The world is your oyster (or in this case your Rice Krispies®). Enjoy!

# EASY-PEASY FAIRY CAKES

My standby recipe for fairy cakes always goes down well in our house. Decorate them with anything and everything you like, from sweets and writing icing to edible glitter, silver and gold balls, hundreds and thousands or firm, seasonal berries. Let your child's inner Jackson Pollock do the decorating.

MAKES: **24**

INGREDIENTS:
- **110g unsalted butter, at room temperature**
- **110g caster sugar**
- **2 large eggs, lightly beaten**
- **1 tsp vanilla extract**
- **110g self-raising flour**
- **2 tbsp milk**

FOR THE ICING:
- **300g icing sugar**
- **3 tbsp unsalted butter, softened**
- **1 tbsp milk or cream**
- **1 tbsp vanilla extract**
- **Food colouring (optional)**

WHAT TO DO:
Preheat the oven to 180°C/Gas 4. Line two 12-cup small muffin or fairy cake/cupcake tins with paper cases or one 24-cup mini muffin tin and place to one side.

To make the cakes, cream the butter and sugar in a large mixing bowl until light and fluffy and beat in the eggs, a little at a time. Stir in the vanilla extract and then add the flour while you continue to beat, a little at a time. Add the milk until the mixture is a soft, dropping consistency.

Divide the batter equally between the paper cases and bake in the preheated oven for about 10 minutes, or until the cakes are a nice light golden brown and spring back to the touch. Remove from the oven and allow to cool in the cases for 10-15 minutes, and then transfer to a wire rack.

To make the icing, sift the icing sugar into a large mixing bowl and mix with all the other ingredients until smooth. Use a mixer if possible to make the icing light and easy to spread. Stir in a drop or two of food colouring if desired. Add a little extra sifted icing sugar to achieve a spreadable consistency if necessary. Use a palette knife or broad butter knife to spread the icing evenly over the top of the cakes in a circular motion. Decorate and serve.

# JAMMY TARTS

You do not need to have any cooking skills to produce these easy tarts. You can, of course, make your own basic pastry with some flour and vegetable fat. I prefer to use the shop-bought stuff and almost always have some to hand.

MAKES: 12

INGREDIENTS:
- Plain flour, for dusting
- 350g packet ready-rolled shortcrust pastry, at room temperature (to prevent it cracking)
- A little unsalted butter or margarine, for greasing
- 1 jar fruit jam or conserve (with high fruit content)

WHAT TO DO:
Preheat the oven to 180°C/Gas 4.

Unfold the pastry on a lightly floured surface or cutting board. Use a round cookie cutter (about 8cm in diameter) to cut out 12 circles. If you find you don't have enough pastry to do this, press the pastry scraps into a ball and roll it out flat. Cut the remaining pastry circles.

Grease the compartments of a 12-cup Yorkshire pudding/shallow muffin tin. Carefully press in the pastry circles so that they reach the top edge with no visible holes. Half fill each one with about 1 tbsp of jam or conserve. Cut out small heart or flower shapes from the leftover pastry to decorate the tops if you like.

Bake in the preheated oven for 20 minutes, or until the edges of the pastry are golden brown and firm. Remove from the oven, cool and serve.

# 144

# DINOSAUR DEVILLED EGGS

These eggs are fun to make, munch on and use as a great party centrepiece. They are an inspiring addition to an enviable packed lunch or picnic and take very little time to prepare, but you will need to allow at least a few hours' soaking time, overnight if possible, in a zip-seal plastic bag.

MAKES: **6-12**

INGREDIENTS:
- **6 large eggs**
- **1 tbsp food colouring**
- **4 tbsp mayonnaise**
- **1 tbsp crème fraîche**
- **¼ tsp mustard powder**
- **¼ tsp dried dill**
- **Salt and freshly ground black pepper, to taste**

WHAT TO DO:
Bring a medium saucepan of water to the boil over medium heat and use a metal spoon to lower the eggs in slowly. Reduce to a simmer and cook for 8-10 minutes. Remove from the water and allow to cool. Once the eggs are cool, dry them with a paper towel and gently tap them on a hard surface until small cracks begin to cover the surface of the shell. Gently squeeze the eggs so that you have a nicely cracked appearance, but try to avoid breaking off pieces of the shell in the process.

Fill a resealable bag half full of tepid water and add the food colouring. Pop the cracked eggs into the bag, seal and refrigerate for several hours. Remove the eggs from the bag, drain the water and gently remove the shells to reveal an amazing dinosaur-egg pattern. You can stop here and serve them whole or go on to devil them as below.

To devil the eggs, carefully cut the eggs in half lengthways and remove the yolks. In a small bowl, mash the yolks and add the mayonnaise, crème fraîche, mustard powder and dill, mixing until smooth. Season to taste. Stir until blended and then scoop the mixture into the egg halves. Serve immediately, before mama dino spots her eggs are missing!

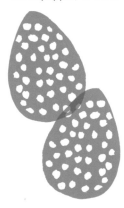

# ANTS ON A LOG

This is an easy, healthy snack that children can make on their own. If peanut butter is not on the menu in your house, use cream cheese instead. The raisins or sultanas become the "ants".

MAKES: **4**

INGREDIENTS:

- **4 celery stalks, washed, topped and tailed**
- **4 tbsp smooth peanut butter (or cream cheese)**
- **4 tbsp raisins or sultanas**

WHAT TO DO:
Simply spread the celery stalks with peanut butter, filling the cavity. Dot the raisins or sultanas over the peanut butter in an ant-like procession, marching along the log, and serve immediately.

MAKES: 8

INGREDIENTS:
- 1 red pepper, washed, de-seeded and cut crossways into 50-mm thick rounds
- 1 yellow pepper, washed, de-seeded and cut crossways into 50-mm thick rounds
- 1 large cucumber, washed and cut lengthways into 50-mm thick strips
- 8 cherry tomatoes
- 4 chive strands, cut into quarters

FOR THE DIP:
- 125ml sour cream
- 2 tbsp mayonnaise
- 1 tsp lemon juice
- Zest of ¼ lemon
- 1 tbsp mixed fresh herbs (dill, parsley, coriander and chives)
- Salt and freshly ground black pepper, to taste

# SWEET PEPPER BUTTERFLIES

These pretty butterflies are a perfect after-school snack or healthy option for birthday party treats. Serve alone or with a creamy dip.

WHAT TO DO:
Place the red and yellow pepper rounds on a large platter and slice them in half to form two wings. Place a strip of cucumber in the centre of each set of wings to form the body. Use a cocktail stick to make two holes in the top half of each cherry tomato, and place a small strand of chive in each to form the butterfly's antennae. Place a cherry tomato head at the top of the cucumber strips.

To make the dip, blend all the ingredients well in a food processor and serve in a pretty bowl in the centre of your flock of butterflies.

Presentation is the key to getting kids to eat. Trust me, I work in show business – it's all about smoke and mirrors! I have plates decorated with faces, on which I arrange "broccoli hair", "tomato earrings" and "pea necklaces". It works every time!

# CHOCOLATE CATERPILLARS

These chocolate and berry caterpillars make a great dessert or party activity. They are simple, no cooking is required and even very young children can make their own with lolly sticks and a little assistance.

MAKES. 4

INGREDIENTS:

- 1 handful miniature medium-sized marshmallows
- 1 handful raspberries, rinsed (as firm as possible)
- 1 handful strawberries, rinsed and hulled
- 1 handful chocolate mini rolls (cut into rounds) or chocolate mini bites
- 4 wooden skewers or lolly sticks
- Black writing icing

WHAT TO DO:
Place the ingredients in bowls and help your children to thread them onto skewers in a pretty pattern, finishing with a marshmallow as the caterpillar's head. Use a blob of writing icing for the eyes.

# JELLY PONDS

Anything goes with these fruity jelly bowls. The aim is to create a jelly "pond", teeming with edible life. Let the wobbly fun begin.

MAKES: **4**

INGREDIENTS:
- **1 packet of green or lime jelly**
- **1 packet of purple or blackcurrant jelly**

WHAT TO DO:

FOR THE POND LIFE: Cut apricot halves into fish shapes, use lettuce, thin cucumber rounds or fresh spinach for lily pads on which rest carrot or melon slices cut into water lily shapes, use pomegranate seeds for frog spawn, mint leaves for foliage, sultanas and raisins for insects, chocolate frogs for . . . frogs!, and add some wriggly jelly worms.

FOR THE POND: Make the blackcurrant jelly according to the packet instructions and pour into four medium-sized glass bowls – you will eventually add the same quantity of lime jelly to each. Place in the refrigerator for about thirty minutes or until the jelly is just beginning to set. Make the lime jelly according to the packet instructions and allow to cool slightly. Pour the lime jelly over the blackcurrant jelly and return to the refrigerator for a further thirty minutes.

When the lime jelly is just beginning to set, it's time to add all the pond life. Press in the fruit gently – the fish shapes may sink to the bottom but your spinach lily pads should rise to the top! Once the pond life has been placed in the jelly, put in the refrigerator for two or three hours, or until set.

# BIRDS NEST TREATS

Now this is my kind of recipe. It's easy, tasty and you can use almost any dry cereal (or even pretzels) to build your nests. These treats are great at Easter or for parties.

MAKES: **12**

INGREDIENTS:
- **200g milk chocolate, in chunks**
- **1 tbsp golden syrup**
- **100g cereal (shredded wheat, Rice Krispies® or corn flakes)**
- **Jelly beans or mini eggs, to decorate**

WHAT TO DO:
Melt the chocolate in a heatproof bowl over a saucepan of just simmering water, stirring frequently until melted. The base of the bowl should sit above the water. Or melt the chocolate in the microwave in a microwave-safe bowl in 30-second bursts, stirring regularly.

Stir in the golden syrup and remove from the heat. Add the cereal and stir until well covered. Spoon into cupcake or muffin cases and press down in the centre with the back of your spoon to create a cavity. Fill with mini eggs, jelly beans or other sweets that look like birds' eggs. Refrigerate for 2 hours, or until set.

# PINK LEMONADE

This traditional American lemonade is extremely refreshing.
It does contain lots of sugar but the number of lemons and
berries in it makes it a nutritious summertime drink. It's a staple
of many a front garden or garden fete "refreshments" stall.

MAKES: 1 large pitcher

INGREDIENTS:
- 2 handfuls of
  strawberries, washed
  and hulled
- 2 handfuls of
  raspberries
- 8–10 lemons (to make
  400ml of juice),
  at room temperature
- 175g superfine
  caster sugar
- Still water, to taste
- Ice
- Sprig of mint

WHAT TO DO:
Either blitz the strawberries and raspberries together in
a food processor or blender until smooth and sieve, or
simply press the fresh berries through a sieve to make
a lovely purée. Don't miss out the sieving stage, whatever
you do! Seeds do not make for a lovely smooth drink.

Roll the lemons firmly on a flat surface before cutting in
half and juicing. You may need to use a few more lemons
to get the required amount of juice. Top up with shop-
bought lemon juice if required, but don't be tempted to
miss out on the fresh lemons. Not only are they sweeter
and more nutritious, but the squeezing is half the fun!

In a tall pitcher, mix together the lemon juice and fruity
purée. Stir in the sugar until dissolved, and then add
water, a little at a time, stirring frequently so that all the
ingredients amalgamate. Pop in some ice cubes, top with
a sprig of mint and serve immediately for the freshest
lemonade you could possibly find.

# RESOURCES

Discount shops, charity shops, supermarkets and even online auctioneers like eBay are often the best way to find the "ingredients" for the projects in this book. You will usually be able to bag a bargain if you buy in bulk and you may be surprised by how quickly you get through your supplies. Below you'll find links that may be of use when planning fun-filled days. Many items are available both online and, where applicable, in-store.

## GENERAL

**Early Learning Centre** www.elc.co.uk
You'll find most things related to children's play here, including dressing-up costumes, child-sized accessories for pretend play, arts and crafts supplies, outdoor toys and furniture, learning games and books, musical games and instruments and more.

**Great Little Trading Co.** www.gltc.co.uk
This is an excellent site for arts and crafts materials (including some good kits), pretend play (kitchens, play food, play houses and wigwams), educational toys, puzzles, and games for both inside and out.

**John Lewis** www.johnlewis.com
Everything from tissue paper, paint, glitter, clothes pegs, felt and glue to scrapbooking accessories, pipe cleaners, jingly bells, googly eyes and pom pom kits can be found here – in-store, head for the haberdashery department. There's also pretend play and dressing-up accessories, learning games and musical toys.

**Littlewoods** www.littlewoods.com
A great range of craft kits and supplies, pretend-play toys, outdoor games and toys, fancy dress, learning toys and even musical instruments. There's also range of games and puzzles for children who like to be busy.

## STORY TIME

**Bookaboo** www.bookaboo.co.uk
Targeted at children between the age of three and six, this site is part of a campaign to promote the idea of adults sharing books with children. Celebrities read their favourite stories, and there are some lovely ones here. Well worth a look, and why not join the Bookaboo club?

**Crafts 4 Kids** www.crafts4kids.co.uk
This company produces a range of pop-up books that children can create themselves, to inspire even the most reluctant little readers.

**DLTK** www.dltk-teach.com/minibooks/
This American site has downloadable sheets that can be bound together to help children create their own books.

**The British Council** www.britishcouncil.org/kids-print-alphabet-dictionary.pdf
Download a wonderful alphabet dictionary to use on flash cards, or visit learnenglishkids.britishcouncil.org/en/category/interactive-types/flashcards for a huge range of flashcards to use in your story-telling activities.

**The Traditional Storyteller** www.traditionalstoryteller.com
Resource site offering apps that feature a storyteller retelling a classic tale (one story per app). Wonderfully engaging.

## MAKING MUSIC

**Children's Music** www.childrensmusic.co.uk
Choose from hundreds of songs, CDs and songbooks, and rhyming picture books, with information on some stringed instruments and advice for parents and teachers. If you are planning to introduce your child to a "proper" instrument (i.e., something a little more formal than an elastic band guitar!), it's always a good idea to get advice from a music teacher.

**Classic FM** www.classicfm.com/hall-of-fame
Classic FM's Hall of Fame is a great place to discover and introduce children to the very best in classical music. It's important to remember that children love all sorts of music, including music that you might consider too adult for them. You might discover some music to inspire you.

Kids Music www.kidsmusic.co.uk
Offering track and album downloads, songbooks, sticker and colouring books with CDs and more, this is a good place to begin introducing music to children. I don't believe that music needs to be made especially for children, but there are some fun collections and things to do here.

National Youth Orchestra www.nyo.org.uk
An amazing group of young people who will undoubtedly inspire your own children with their talent. Definitely worth a look to see a performance and inspire budding talent.

Story Time Songs
www.storytimesongs.com/activities
A lovely website offering plenty of ideas for games based on music, instruments to make at home, and lyrics and guitar chords for children's songs. Fairy tale song CDs are also available.

The Vegetable Orchestra
www.vegetableorchestra.org
An entire orchestra of instruments made from vegetables! Inspire children to make their own musical experiments with vegetables and perhaps get to know a few new ones in the process.

## ARTS AND CRAFTS

Baker Ross www.bakerross.co.uk
This site is excellent value for craft materials and has a huge range of paint, card, paint pens for glass and porcelain, feathers, Cellophane, glitter and glitter pens, ribbons, stickers, stamps, tissue paper, clay, wooden craft sticks, drawing paper rolls and more.

Beads Direct www.beadsdirect.co.uk
Visit this site for beads and buttons of all descriptions, as well as stretchy cord, sequins, ribbon, paint, glue, charms, tiara bases, and resin clay and tools.

Little Crafty Bugs www.littlecraftybugs.co.uk
Craft supplies of every description are reasonably priced here, including bulk purchases, scrapbooks, frames and themed crafts (i.e., Halloween and Christmas). Plenty of craft ideas, too.

Moonstone Craft Supplies
www.moonstonecraftsupplies.co.uk
Moonstone specialises in children's arts and crafts supplies, with a huge range of materials, ideas for activities and projects, kits and more.

## GREEN FINGERS

Farm Toys Online www.farmtoysonline.co.uk
You'll find great gardening tools for little hands, and lovely seed kits, including one for a fairy garden. It's also a good source of miniature toys for pretend play.

Kids in the Garden www.kidsinthegarden.co.uk
A good source of information for anyone interested in gardening with children. It offers advice on family-friendly plants, when and how to plant seeds, plant care, "edible" gardens, etc. They also sell seeds, growing kits, tools and outdoor toys such as a chalkboard roll mat.

Spotty Green Frog www.spottygreenfrog.co.uk
This site has everything from composting sets for children to tools, butterfly and bee feeding stations, earthworm farms, paper pot makers and vegetable and fruit plants.

Unwins www.unwins.co.uk
This long-established firm sells an excellent range of easy-to-grow seeds for children.

## OUTDOOR PLAY

Bill Oddie's Bird Food Recipes
www.billoddiesbirdfood.co.uk
A lovely site with lots of recipe ideas for bird foods to make at home, including bird cakes and honey sticks.

Team Magnus www.team-magnus.co.uk
This is a great online shop for all things outdoors, including a variety of different pavement chalks, outdoor wear and useful tools for outdoor projects. Search for "Sorted for". They also offer lots of ideas for activities.

The Kids Window www.thekidswindow.co.uk
This company sells good quality outdoor games and toys, including kites, sandpits, water tables, sprinklers, play houses, gardening materials and seeds, tents and plenty of things that could be used to create the perfect obstacle course.

## INDOOR PLAY

Crafty Kids www.craftykids.co.uk
A site selling kits for all kinds of puppets at reasonable prices.

Kids Love Fancy Dress
www.kidslovefancydress.co.uk
A highly original site offering themed fancy dress, from historical (Victorian urchins and Crusader

knights, etc.) to pirates, book, film and TV characters, and modern occupations. Reasonable prices for avid dresser-uppers.
Maudesport www.maudesport.com
Although this is a huge site, with tools and equipment for almost every sport imaginable, there are some treasures here, in particular, the unbelievably wide range of beanbags on offer, which can be bought on their own or in bulk. Lots of fun ideas for indoor (and outdoor) fun.
Mothercare www.mothercare.com
Mothercare sells fantastic costumes for dressing up and toys for pretend play. Everything from kitchen sets, cash registers, supermarket checkouts and trolleys, to play food, vacuum cleaners and ironing boards, cleaning sets and laundry centres.
Pretend to Bee www.pretendtobee.co.uk
I'm pretty sure that every single interest and eventuality is covered here. The biggest selection of dressing-up costumes for children that I've ever seen, including figures from history, animals, fairies, dinosaurs, book characters, pretend play "professions", and much, much more.
Puppets By Post www.puppetsbypost.com
If you'd like a kit to make your own puppets or prefer to buy them ready-made, or if you're on the lookout for a puppet stage or theatre, this is the place to go.
Snazaroo www.snazaroo.com
One of the leading names in face paints, Snazaroo sells them on their site and has advice on getting started and step-by-step instructions on how to achieve lots of different character faces.

## LEARNING GAMES

BBC School Radio
www.bbc.co.uk/schoolradio/subjects/
earlylearning/nurserysongs
Download nursery rhymes and songs as mp3 files or listen to them on the spot. Many have nice little animations that will help to entertain your child while you learn the words (and possibly actions) together.
Family Learning www.familylearning.org.uk
You'll find plenty of safe, fun and effective online games to encourage maths, literacy and other skills on this site. It covers virtually every age group and provides links to other useful sites.

Just Childsplay www.justchildsplay.co.uk
There are plenty of learning games to be found here, including memory games, travel games, water play, pretend play, puppets, letters and numbers games, painting sponges, puzzles, books and stories, and sorting games.
Mulberry Bush www.mulberrybush.co.uk
This site is a good source for educational and craft toys, games, puzzles, and history and geography games, such as Flags of the World (and globes). It also sells lovely baking sets for children.
Topmarks www.topmarks.co.uk
Topmarks offers songs and rhymes for children, with lyrics that can be printed out, animation and music to download. It's a great place to start if you aren't familiar with traditional (and not so traditional) favourites.

## IN THE KITCHEN

BBC – recipes to bake with children
www.bbc.co.uk/food/collections/baking_with_
children
These are easy-to-follow recipes for savoury and sweet treats to make with your child.
Cake Craft Shop www.cakecraftshop.co.uk
Buy gel food colouring, sugarpaste, and all sorts of decorations and baking equipment from this vast site.
Lakeland www.lakeland.co.uk
Everything you need to cook with kids can be found here, including cake and cookie decorations (and the equipment to make them), moulds and cookware and bakeware, glycerine for home-made bubbles, corn skewers, cake pop sticks for safely skewering kebabs, and food colouring.
National Baking Week
www.nationalbakingweek.co.uk/baking-kids
This is a great resource with explanations of techniques, lists of essential equipment and lots of child-friendly recipes.
The Kids Cooking Company
www.thekidscookingcompany.co.uk
This site sells a good range of baking and decorating equipment, including cookware, aprons, cutters, as well as ready-made decorations. There are also recipes to download.

# ACTIVITY LIST

# INDEX

Text © Myleene Klass 2013
Design and layout © Orion Publishing Group 2013
Photography © Tara Moore 2013, except photographs below
Shutterstock: 138, 155, 163 (top left, bottom), 167, 185, 200 (top right)

First published in Great Britain in 2013 by Orion Books
This paperback edition published in Great Britain in 2014 by
Orion Books
an imprint of the Orion Publishing Group Ltd
Orion House, 5 Upper St Martin's Lane,
London WC2H 9EA
An Hachette UK Company

10 9 8 7 6 5 4 3 2 1

**Editorial:** Jane Sturrock, Nicola Crossley, Jackie Strachan and Jane Moseley
**Consultant:** Karen Sullivan
**Art direction and design:** Nikki Dupin for nicandlou
**Photographer:** Tara Moore
**Illustrator:** Jenny Bowers
**Proofreader:** Laura Nickoll
**Indexer:** Elizabeth Wiggans

ISBN: 978 1 4091 2691 1

Printed and bound in China

www.orionbooks.co.uk